The New
Rules of
Divorce

The New Rules of Divorce

Twelve Secrets to Protecting Your Wealth, Health, and Happiness

Jacqueline Newman

ATRIA PAPERBACK

New York   London   Toronto   Sydney   New Delhi

ATRIA
PAPERBACK

An Imprint of Simon & Schuster, Inc.
1230 Avenue of the Americas
New York, NY 10020

First Atria Books Paperback edition January 2022

ATRIA PAPERBACK and colophon are
trademarks of Simon & Schuster, Inc.

For information about special discounts for bulk purchases, please contact Simon & Schuster Special Sales at 1-866-506-1949 or business@simonandschuster.com.

The Simon & Schuster Speakers Bureau can bring authors to your live event. For more information or to book an event, contact the Simon & Schuster Speakers Bureau at 1-866-248-3049 or visit our website at www.simonspeakers.com.

Interior design by Jill Putorti

Manufactured in the United States of America

1 3 5 7 9 10 8 6 4 2

Library of Congress Cataloging-in-Publication Data has been applied for.

ISBN 978-1-9821-2793-0
ISBN 978-1-9821-2794-7 (pbk)
ISBN 978-1-9821-2795-4 (ebook)

To My Parents:
Thank you for teaching me the skill to be
able to listen to people and actually hear them.

In memory of Len Lipson—
I know you would have liked this.

CONTENTS

INTRODUCTION

Who gets married? Starry-eyed kids in their twenties. Starry-eyed kids in their forties. Boomers. Millennials. The young. The old. The old who want to feel young. The rich. The poor, the just-scraping-by. Men and women. Men and men. Women and women. The workaholic. The shopaholic. The alcoholic. Your cousin. Your best friend. Your ex. Brenda and Eddie from that Billy Joel song. Billy Joel.

Who gets divorced? Starry-eyed kids in their twenties. Starry-eyed kids in their forties. Boomers. Millennials. The young. The old. The old who want to feel young. The rich. The poor, the just-scraping-by. Men and women. Men and men. Women and women. The workaholic. The shopaholic. The alcoholic. Your cousin. Your best friend. Brenda and Eddie from that Billy Joel song. Billy Joel.

People get married, and people get divorced. If you know anything about statistics—or people—this is not a surprising fact. And it has been going on forever, in some form or another. One of the oldest known marriage breakups in history was that of Henry VIII and Catherine of Aragon in 1527. Henry wanted to annul his marriage to Catherine (because she did not produce a male heir) to marry the younger, prettier Anne Boleyn (the first noted version of the male midlife crisis). Then when Anne could not produce a male either (Henry did not like to look in the mirror much), he decided that instead of divorcing her, he would behead her instead.

So divorce (in some form) has been around for almost five hundred years. However, over time things have changed and continue to change. Courthouses have replaced guillotines, and you now can get divorced (if you want) basically because you do not like the way he* crunches his cereal.

While I am a matrimonial attorney** (and have been for the past twenty years), I am still a romantic at heart. Even though I see marriages break up every day, I believe that everyone can find someone to be happy with. But I am also realistic enough to know that that "someone" may or may not be your current spouse. It could be your spouse, or the guy you meet on the Starbucks line tomorrow morning, or the girl you meet at yoga class next week, or maybe it is simply the "someone" you see in the mirror. So one of the goals of this book is to help you figure who your "someone" is.

Now, if it is concluded after completing chapter 2 (Secret #2: You May Not Be Ready to Get Divorced) that your someone is not your current spouse (or if your spouse made that decision for you), then the next goal here is to provide you with the practical guidance necessary to be prepared for that shift in your life. Think of this book as the *What to Expect When You're Expecting*—or not expecting—for divorce.

However, I do want to warn you that this book is not going to sugarcoat and may seem harsh at times, but let's face it—the divorce process is not fun, and I would be doing you a disservice to pretend that it was. My tone can be pretty direct, and I really do not bullshit. Since I feel I owe it to my clients to be honest, I also owe honesty to you. So if there are parts

---

*In this book, I tend to take the point of view of the Wife referring to the soon-to-be-ex as a male. However, in most situations you can change the roles and pronouns as needed given your circumstances.

**Yes, a "matrimonial attorney" is the same thing as a "divorce lawyer," I just think it sounds nicer.

of this book that hit too close to home and may make you cry—that's okay and perfectly normal (I considered printing this book in plastic to protect against tearstains). But I am hoping there may also be a few lines in here that make you laugh a little too (or at least crack a smile).

I wrote this book for two reasons, and they may at first seem contradictory, but stick with me for a bit. One goal is to encourage the people who are feeling frustrated and bored in their marriages to think twice before falling into the "grass is always greener" syndrome. I want to catch the midlife crisis early and tell people that they should not end their marriage because sex is always missionary style (when you even have it) and you literally would rather read a Chinese menu than listen to your husband drone on about his workday. I want people who stare at Facebook (or whatever social media platform that is cool at the time you are reading this) and think that every other couple on there (even your archnemesis from high school) seem to be so schmoopy, to realize that the second after the picture was taken, the wife is screaming at the husband about the fact that he was sleeping with her (ex–) best friend. I want people to realize that marriage is tough and there is no such thing as picture-perfect. If someone tells you that they are still always gaga over their husband after twelve years of marriage, two kids, and a mortgage to pay, that person is probably lying to you (cynical, I know—but also realistic). Marriage is often boring and annoying and monotonous and all the fun words in between. So while I am a divorce lawyer and this advice goes directly against my profit margins—I want some of the people who read this book to not get divorced and never call me and never pay my consultation fee. I would consider it a success if you finish reading and right after you turn the last page, go have non-missionary sex with your husband.

However, I am not writing to tell you to stay married either. Did you know that in 2016, there were 6.9 marriages in the United States for every 1,000 people and 3.2 divorces per every 1,000 people—that means that 46 percent of the marriages ended in divorce (which is often rounded up to 50 percent)?[1] The typical marriage in the United States that ends in divorce only lasts seven years (so if you made it past seven years, you are beating the national average). Therefore, if you are part of the 50 percent–ish of couples who are getting divorced, I want you to know that I have seen thousands of clients in a worse state than you are (after twenty years of matrimonial practice, I do not even need to know your situation to say that), and they have survived and are often happier after. Divorce is not the end of your world (despite how it may feel right now) and can be seen as a beginning instead. I promise that you will come out on the other end of this process and (if done properly) may even be better for it. Let's face it—very few mammals mate for life. I believe it is time to normalize divorce (I know I will get some serious backlash for that), because anything that has a little more than a 50 percent chance of survival should fall within the realm of normal. At this point, it is almost as normal to get divorced as it is to stay married. After you turn the last page of this book, the goal is for you to feel confident and good (as good as you can) about the turn your life is taking. To know that *you've got this*.

In life, I believe in making rational, thought-out, and educated decisions. People think that because I am a divorce attorney I try to push divorce on people (I promise I do not solicit at weddings). However, that is simply not true. If you have gone through the proper analysis of your marriage and concluded that you are getting divorced for the right reasons (not because you do not like the way your husband crunches his cereal), then I support that conclusion and, at that point, want to help you to be strategic, analytical, and smart about the way you move forward.

The idea to write a book came to me when I had this client—let's call her Blake*—come to see me a few years ago. I really liked this client (*not*

---

*Names and any identifying details of all clients cited in this book have been changed to protect the clients' identities and attorney/client privilege (and not to worry future clients that their story may end up in a book one day).

that I do not like all my clients), but she and I really clicked (like we would have been part of the same friend group if we went to high school together). Blake had what I considered to be a very typical story for the clients I represent in New York City. She was married to a successful man who worked on Wall Street. They had three young children in private school (at $55,000+ per year a pop).* Blake also had previously worked in finance (where she had met her husband) and was earning a pretty good living before she stopped working to raise their children. Her husband was a good father (when he was around) but did not really get involved with day-to-day parenting. She started a small jewelry business with a few friends out of her apartment that was getting some headway, but she did not really have the time to dedicate to it because she was busy taking one kid uptown to soccer practice, while rushing to get back to pick up Kid #2 from therapy and coordinating with her nanny to get the littler one from a playdate downtown. Blake talked about how she had been thinking of getting divorced for years because while her husband was not abusive, he was kind of an asshole. He would insult her in front of the children and belittle her contributions to the marriage as a homemaker and mother. They were no longer having sex (her choice) and he was putting her on a strict financial budget (although he made millions a year). She told me she saw an attorney years ago when she first thought of divorcing him and that attorney scared the shit out of her about what the process would entail and was so über aggressive, she thought that if he was indicative of what other men were like out there—her husband may not be that bad! (Kind of ironic that seeing a divorce attorney resulted in her staying married.)

Blake talked about when she and her husband would fight, he would threaten that if she divorced him, she would not see a dime of support and that he would take the kids from her because she would not be able

---

*This family is similar to my Manhattan clients. I would like to note that even if your family income levels are not on par with this case, the issues remain universal.

to afford to stay in the city and the court would want the kids to stay in their home and in their schools. She talked about being nervous about how much he would "give" her of the marital assets. She sheepishly admitted that she really knew little of their financial situation because that was not her arena in the marriage.

Blake also spoke of how she did not want her children to grow up in a broken home and felt she owed it to them to make the marriage work. She was honest enough (which is one of the reasons I liked her so much) to acknowledge that part of the reason she stayed married was simply inertia and exhaustion. If she did not have the energy to make it to her 7:30 a.m. spin class, how could she muster the strength to go through with a divorce?

The reason that Blake was in my office was because her husband had an affair and got caught. Ironically, she was not even looking for signs (I am not sure she was interested enough to snoop), but it was the ole "text messages popping up when the phone was on the kitchen counter" syndrome. Gets 'em every time (just ask Spitzer, Weiner, and Woods).

So Blake was being forced to do something because he knew she knew about the affair, and while he was denying it, she knew it happened. The joke of it is that she was not even sure she cared that he was sleeping around but more that she was being lied to and felt like a fool. So she wanted to know what she should do and thus came to see me for a Divorce 101 lesson and a strategic lawyering session.

I have seen dozens and dozens of scenarios that are similar to Blake's. Sure, there are variances—sometimes there are two kids, not three; sometimes the wife has the affair; sometimes the wife is not the stay-at-home mom (but still usually hears the threats of losing her kids); sometimes the guy is not a cheating asshole, but she really has just outgrown the marriage; sometimes it is a mutual agreement between the spouses to end it—the list goes on. But the fears and the themes remain similar in so many cases, and I find that I am repeating similar advice to clients all the time. I thought it was time that I put all the words of wisdom I have been repeating for years in one place that would hopefully provide some insight to people facing this change in their lives.

Even if your fact pattern does not match that of Blake's, you still probably have concerns about your children and your finances. You still need to understand the basics of divorce before you set out on this path, and I want to help you if you are in the financial dark. So many people have such misconceptions about the divorce process and believe all they see on TV and what their best friend's neighbor's cousin's uncle's brother told them. I am writing to shed a little light on the realities of divorce and provide an insider's view into the divorce process.

In this book I will dispense some of the divorce secrets I have accumulated over the years and:

- help you understand how the changes in our society have impacted divorce over the past ten to twenty years;

- make you question whether you are ready to get divorced, and if so, figure out the best timing;

- provide you with Divorce 101, which covers different process choices, asset division, support, and custody;

- discuss abusive marriages and what to do to protect yourself;

- provide tools to help you select the best attorney for you;

- teach strategies as how to best play the game of psychological chess when negotiating (which can be more important than the law itself);

- help you protect your kids in this process;

- paint a picture for you of what your life may look like before, during, and after the divorce; and finally

- show you that there are some serious perks to divorce!

This book will provide you with the strategies to help you be able to end your marriage in a more humane and economically savvy way.

I must also warn you as a reader that I do not hate men, so this is not going to be a man-hating book. I will definitely be making a few jokes at the expense of the penis people on the planet, but that will be the extent of it. I do represent both men and women, and depending on the day, I could even be representing more men than women at a given time. I think that provides me an edge when representing either sex, as I have seen behind the iron curtain and have a good understanding of what concerns both men and women typically have when facing divorce. I can get into their heads. I want to bring women up without putting men down—hopefully I can accomplish this.

To be clear: **Reading this book will not replace meeting with an attorney!** But hopefully it will give you a baseline to make your conversations with your attorney as efficient as possible (attorneys do bill by the hour after all, and I can tell you that the cost of the book in your hands is cheaper than probably fifteen minutes of your attorney's time).

With all this said, let's discuss the secrets of divorce. This book is for the Blakes out there, as well as any Jessicas, Kellys, Heathers, Samanthas, Alexandras, and all roses by other names. Time to figure out who is your "someone."

The New Rules of Divorce

SECRET #1

Divorce, Like Marriage,
Is a New World with New Rules

Step out of the history that is holding you back.
Step into the new story you are willing to create.
—OPRAH WINFREY

Gone are the days of the traditional housewife bringing a shaken martini to her husband when he walks in the door from work. While we are not yet at the point of most men bringing their wives a French martini when she walks in the door—it could be around the corner.

The old defaults about who stays home with the kids and who brings home the bacon are no longer so bedrock. While women still earn only 78 percent of what their husbands earn (which has increased from 52 percent in 1970),[1] there are more and more women earning more than their husbands.* A study from the Bureau of Labor Statistics states that in the United States 29 percent of women outearn their husbands in dual-income homes, which is up from 23 percent in the 1990s and 18 percent in the 1980s.[2] If you also consider marriages where the wife is the sole financial provider, the percentage increases to 38 percent.[3] When I first started practicing about two decades ago, I probably had one or

---

*This stat does not include America's cohabitating couples, which are estimated to be 6.5 million of opposite sex and 700,000 of same sex.

two female clients who outearned their husbands (and at the time I was so impressed).* Now, I would estimate that about 35 to 40 percent of my female clients earn similar if not more money than their husbands. Talk to me in ten years, I am guessing we will be at 80 percent or higher. The trend is going in the right direction, and women are no longer being assumed to be the default caregivers, and the role of stay-at-home dad has become more normalized (remember when we called that "Mr. Mom"?).

Last week, while I was working from home one day and I had to do what felt like (and may have actually been) one thousand errands for my two daughters (while balancing conference calls and dealing with closing my firm's year-end books before tax time), I jokingly said to my husband (who had the luxury of focusing on just work that day), I feel like "Mr. Mom today." He said back to me "Isn't that just Mom?" While Mrs. Dad does not have the same ring to it, the phrase SAHD (stay-at-home dad) has grown in popularity and was made official by an Urban Dictionary entry.[4] The celebrity world has supported this movement, with fathers making it very public that they are fine being the primary caretakers for their children, while their wives are out working. Look at John Lennon, who stayed home with son Sean from 1975 to 1980 and proudly referred to himself as a "househusband."

Courts have also noticed that there are more women in the workplace and therefore are now assuming that women are capable of earning income outside the home, even if they spent their married years within it. This revelation by our justice system is evidencing itself in the shifting of alimony / maintenance / spousal support** laws. Courts rarely award lifetime spousal support awards anymore. And the amounts awarded are lowering as well. So in this day and age, the exchange of a JD degree for

---

*It should be noted that I practice in New York City, and as a female attorney, it could account for why my percentage is higher than the national average.

**All the same thing, by the way.

an "MRS degree" is a risky move. If a woman has the degree and stops working, a court could look to her and say that she has the ability to earn and may give somewhat short shrift to the fact that the only briefs she has been dealing with for the past five years are in the form of diapers.

DAMNED IF YOU DO, DAMNED IF YOU DON'T

A University of Chicago study found that of the four thousand US married couples they looked at, when the wife was the higher earner, the chances that the couple would report being in a "happy marriage" fell by 6 percent.[5] While the train is leaving the station with workingwomen on it, not all societal norms are on board. The courts seem to want women to work, but not all men do (except when they are arguing that they should not have to pay spousal support). Fewer and fewer people feel that women should stay home, but there is still this general consensus that the men should be the providers. Another study found that men who were entirely financially dependent on their female partners are five times more likely to cheat.[6] However, the more financially dependent a woman is on her husband, the less likely she is to cheat. But if the husband makes much more money than his wife, he is also more likely to cheat. Christin Munsch, the study's author, noted, "At one end of the spectrum, making less money than a female partner may threaten men's gender identity by calling into question the traditional notion of men as breadwinners. At the other end of the spectrum, men who make a lot more money than their partners may be in jobs that offer more opportunities for cheating like long work hours, travel and higher incomes making cheating easier to conceal."[7]

So, many men are obviously insecure when their wives earn more money than they do. However, women do not help this situation when they play into their reindeer games. According to a study done by Marta Murray-Close and Misty L. Heggeness in June 2018,[8] when the women in relationships who earn higher incomes than their partners report their income to the US Census Bureau, they tend to want to lessen the gap between income levels. A woman will report income to the bureau that is 1.5 percentage points lower on average than her actual income (as reported on her tax returns) while the income for her spouse is reported at 2.9 percentage points higher.* However, this discrepancy does not occur when a man outearns the woman (because then everything feels right in the world).[9]

Women outearning men is part of the new world we live in, and men need to get used to it. As comedian Ali Wong said, "Now I make a lot more money than my husband. My mom is very concerned that he is going to leave me out of intimidation. I had to explain to her that the only kind of man that would leave a woman who makes more money is the kind of man who doesn't like free money."[10]

WOMEN CAN DO ANYTHING—BUT DOES THAT MEAN THEY HAVE TO DO EVERYTHING?

Women have been upsetting all the apple carts since the dawn of time (hi, Eve and the apple), but since we're not quite at full, blanket equality, it always tends to feel like we are in the throes of change and progress. (And not for nothing, that tension undergirds some of our favorite TV shows and movies—*The Good Wife, Game of Thrones, Madam Secretary, VEEP,* and—this could be controversial, but bear with me—*Grease 2.* It wasn't an accident that the sequel focused on the fearless, independent Stephanie Zinone fighting for her freedom of choice. "I wanted to ask if you're free after school today?" asks Michael Carrington, her hapless suitor. "Yeah, I'm free every day," Stephanie replies. "It's in the Constitution.") Independent women, shaking the foundations—same fight, different decade.

But while doors have opened to women in many facets of the job market, the door has not fully closed on the roles that they assumed from

---

*This seems to stay consistent whether the husband or wife is answering the survey.

years past. Women still tend to do the lion's share of the household labor and carry the brunt of the mental load. In fact, a study from the University of Chicago Booth School of Business states that American women spend forty-four minutes more on housework a day than men do, and the gap is even larger for women who earn more than their husbands.[11] WTF?!

Having phrases like "mental load" is an acknowledgment that emotional labor counts as, well, labor—and that women are far more likely to be saddled with it. Does this count in divvying up assets or establishing custody? Not explicitly—but it's a factor, and since *Price v. Price*[12] in 1986 (New York), the indirect and nonfinancial contributions of a spouse "as homemaker and parent" are considered to be of value and weighed in determining equitable distribution of property.

DO THEY EVEN MAKE
WHITE PICKET FENCES ANYMORE?

Women's growing presence in the workforce is not the only factor that is changing the family dynamic and therefore changing the landscape of divorce. The so-called traditional family is no longer the default either—gay marriage is now legal and becoming commonplace; kids are born to unmarried cohabitating partners[13] (and often their parents have different names whether they are married or not); children are resulting from short-lived unions, leading to awkward co-parenting scenarios; there are mommies and daddies, but there may not be one mommy, or one daddy, or everyone in question may just be a nonbinary them/they; families are blending and, in some cases, splitting and blending again. The new normal is a spectrum of normal.

Courts are aware of the change in the family structure, and regardless of how many mommies are involved, it is no longer a given that the mothers (or whomever the primary custodial parent is) will get full custody of the kids. I know this may be hard to hear if you are one of those who have dedicated your every breathing moment to these smaller humans (but it may also be music to your ears if your kids are teenagers). These days fathers (and/or nonprimary parents) are more likely to want—and demand—equal custody of their children, even if they have not been the primary caregiver thus far. Fifteen years ago, a man who walked into my office and asked for fifty-fifty time with his children would have been met with a chuckle and the requirement that, unless his wife beats their children with whips while snorting coke off their Elmo dinner plates, there was no way he was getting fifty-fifty custody. However, today the story is so much different. It is fair to say that, depending on the age of the child or children, as well as geography and some other factors, fifty-fifty custody is slowly becoming the new default position for parents living in the same city. This is not the position for every judge, and it's certainly not happening in every state (red states are least likely to have equal-split time, and a swing state is more likely to make time equal).[14] However, parenting schedules are more nuanced and favor the assumption that parenting time for fathers is weighted similarly as parenting time for mothers. Give it another five to ten years and it will be the burden of the primary parent to show why it is *not* in the best interests of the child to spend equal time with both parents.

I have seen firsthand the shift in the court's attitude. When I was only a couple of years into practice, I remember representing a father—let's call him Evan—who traveled a ton for work and spent 80 percent of his waking hours at the office and admittedly did not see his two children much during the week. But he loved these kids. He would tell me how he would come home late from work and just go into his children's rooms to watch them sleep as he took such comfort in them being safe and happy. His wife was what was stereotypically referred to as an "Upper East Side Barbie" who lived the high life with two nannies (one-to-one ratio) and lunched and shopped and did everything you would think she would do. Enter the tennis pro (cliché, I know) which resulted in Evan's entering my office. While money was a concern, that dulled in comparison to his concern that he would not be able to maintain a serious role in his children's lives. Unfortunately, while we negotiated the case the judge was very clear that because he worked so much and was rarely home, his time with the children would be limited to every other weekend and Wednesday dinners. The judge also unabashedly stated that she believed that children should be with their mother. My client was fully distraught, but, in those days, there was not much that could be done. We did get him some midweek overnights (which was a win back then) and extra time in the summers, and he had more of the holidays than his wife (who did not care much, as the tennis pro also had off for the holidays). While the court appreciated this guy worked to support his family, in the end, his working as hard as he did screwed him when it came to his kids.

More recently, I represented another father—let's call him Matthew—who had a similar story—long hours, travel, weekend bonding time with the kids, etc. He walked into my office and wanted almost equal time with his children (he recognized that a full fifty-fifty was not doable because of his work hours). We spoke about his work schedule, and he felt that he could minimize his travel and when he did travel, that he could do it on Thursdays/Fridays, which would result in his being able to be home on Mondays. The mother in this case felt strongly that she did not believe he could manage such a schedule (after all, why didn't he do that when they were married?) and told the court that he was bluffing. The judge did not care. The judge took the position that she was going to give this father the chance to be with his children as much as he could be and was not going to let the history dictate the future. The judge was adamant that Matthew be granted a schedule that gave him significant and consistent time with his children. I think back to my first client and wonder if he got divorced now, how differently his case may have turned out. Bottom line: the "every-other-weekend and Wednesday dinner" dad is looking more and more like a thing of the past.

AS THE WHITE-PICKET-FENCE BUSINESS SUFFERS, THE DIVORCE INDUSTRY REMAINS ALIVE AND WELL

Although getting divorced is not new, there are new ways to get divorced. Divorce is no longer the *Kramer vs. Kramer* template some of us grew up with—as there are a multitude of ways to get to the dotted line, with varying degrees of expense. No longer do you need to always "duke it out in court." There are an overwhelming number of process choices and ways to get divorced, more than ever before (mediation, collaborative law, kitchen-table negotiations, old-fashioned litigation are all options). Gone are the days of divorce simply being "one size fits all."

Divorce has also become a team sport, and it is no longer just two lawyers sitting in the room. Many divorces nowadays can involve an army of middlemen—parenting coordinators, divorce coaches (a.k.a. divorce doula), divorce accountants, child specialists, child therapists, adult therapists, custody forensics, forensic accountants, private investigators, etc. And now the technology field is taking a bite of the divorce apple and there are a ton of websites and a multitude of apps that can assist along the way. While all of these experts may have you seeing green, if used properly, they can actually be cost savers because most of them will likely have lower billable rates than your attorney.

Even the process of how you pre-divorce has gotten some Madison Avenue attention. While you are in the midst of divorcing (or sometimes even after) some couples will "nest." Nesting is when your children stay in the marital home and the parents rotate in and out. There are mixed views on nesting, as some schools of thought say it is confusing for the children while other experts say it is a nice way to transition the children into being parented by one parent at a time without too much disruption. Nesting is sometimes financially necessary when your marital home is your most expensive asset and you do not have the means to replicate the housing situation for the children. It also can make sense if the real estate market is not your friend and it is a bad time to sell. Oftentimes nesting can be a good option if the couple has not figured out the parenting-access schedule yet and neither wants to leave the apartment (and weaken any custody positions) but yet the only thing they do agree on is that they do not want to live together. Often when nesting, the parties will get another smaller apartment and the non-nesting parent will live there when it is not his/her days in the marital residence. The problem with nesting is that it does not give either spouse any of his or her "own space." One of the things you may be excited about in connection with not living with your spouse anymore is that you no longer have to smell his nauseating cologne or clean his toothpaste scum out of the sink. Well, if you are still living in the same quarters (albeit not at the same time), and divorcing simultaneously, he is most likely not going to make efforts to put the toilet seat down. Many of my clients can afford to get two separate apartments, which is ideal but very expensive because they are then maintaining three residences (while paying legal bills). So, assuming one cannot afford three residences, nesting is not usually a long-term solution but can be a stopgap during the divorce proceedings. The most common complaint I get about nesting from clients is: "But I don't want to sleep in a different bed every night." When I hear that, I take a few seconds to look at my client square in the eye and say, "But you think your kids do?"

There is also now "conscious uncoupling"—made famous by Gwyneth Paltrow and Chris Martin—which can come off as very nice and peaceful (hopefully it will be). This involves (as I understand it) the respectful and amicable separation that allows the marital relationship to dissolve but transform into a new friendship. From what I have read about Gwyneth and Chris's divorce, it does seem that they were able to end their relationship with respect, and even if they didn't, they managed to play it to the media as if they did, and so their children never need to read about the details of their parents' divorce—which is enough to get kudos from me.

THE NOT-QUITE-SCARLET "D"

Divorce has come with an invisible burden of stigma and shame, often weighted down with feelings of failure and sadness. (Saying goodbye to a life-encircling partnership is not nothing—that will always be true.) But the stigma that existed of yesterday is just not true of today. Thanks to cultural shifts and sheer commonality (anything in the neighborhood of 50 percent is a nontrivial percentage), being divorced is no scarlet letter, and being a divorcée doesn't make you a Hester Prynne. Even Catholics are coming around—an estimated 28 percent of Catholic marriages end in divorce,[15] which is lower than the national rate but probably higher than the Church would like. (Not that the Church didn't see this coming, since even the Catechism calls divorce "contagious.")[16] But where marriage is concerned—that monolithic, all-encompassing institution that is, in fact, made up of individual people in individual couplings—freedom of choice has been the clincher. Because when people are free to choose their own destiny . . . they do, and women should not feel bad, guilty, or like a horrible person for doing so.

Divorce can actually be an incredibly appealing choice when compared to staying in a bad marriage. Independence. Autonomy. Self-determination. Freedom from a partner who is not, in the real sense anymore, a partner. Whether it's your choice or not, from this point on you, at least, get to choose how to go forward. It may not be easy, it may not be fun, and—sorry—it will likely be expensive. (I can't pretend to sugarcoat that.) But it's your life, and this book is meant to give you all the tools to go forward with it with as much freedom and possibility as the world has to offer. Let's get you ready for it.

You May Not Be
Ready to Get Divorced

The most difficult thing is the decision to act.
The rest is mere tenacity.
—AMELIA EARHART

Before anything, you need to first figure out if you actually want to get divorced. Therefore, the first question I ask any client who walks into my office is, "Are you sure you want to get divorced?" If they hesitate for even a second, I tell them to go consult with a therapist.

Why did I just tell a potential paying client to leave my office? Because divorce is not fun. It is emotionally and financially exhausting. You need to be sure this is what you want to do before you go down this path. It is not an easy thing to come back from, and you want to be sure you have done whatever you can to save the marriage before taking this life-altering step. While life is full of regrets (and the marriage to your spouse might be one of them), you do not want to ever second-guess your decision to divorce.

TOUGH QUESTIONS TO PONDER

Think back to when you and your spouse were only dating. Remember those idyllic days? You were in love, in lust, infatuated with each other.

11

The future was wide open with wonderful possibilities. And you were thinking marriage.

Now, I am assuming you did not enter into your marriage on a whim. Most people, after all, truly assess their potential partner's character and qualities as a mate. *Is he breeding material? Does he want kids? What shared goals do you have? What do your individual and shared finances look like? What are his attitudes about work?* The list was probably extensive. So the same thing goes now as you contemplate exiting your marriage. Here are some questions you should also think about as you look to make an educated and rational decision regarding divorce—and answer them truthfully:

- Have you spoken to your spouse about your feelings? What was the reaction?

- Has marriage counseling been suggested? If so, what was the result?

- Has time been taken to discuss the problems within the marriage and isolate their causes?

- Is there an open line of communication? Or do your conversations result in nagging, arguing, or even tuning each other out?

- Are the two of you able to compromise and find a happy medium?

- Taking away the stresses of the day, are you able to enjoy downtime together?

- Has there been a recent change that has caused stress within the marriage? (For example, job loss; change in financial situation; new baby; death of a parent, sibling or close friend.) These are all major behavioral triggers and suggest that your spouse may just need time and support before coming through to the other side.

- Are you able to kiss and make up? Are you able to break the tension with a joke? Do either or both of you hold grudges?

- When you fight (and all married couples do) is it productive so that a compromise or negotiation is reached? Or is it personal and dirty?

- Do you have a history of being able to work on issues together?

Thoroughly weigh your options if you believe your marriage is over before simply assuming that divorce is the healthiest and best choice. And while you are thinking it over, why not think about this celebrity couple who has shown us time and time again that marriage is complex and durable: Ozzy and Sharon Osbourne. They have separated so many times; they talk divorce and then they seem to always work it out. They have admitted to seeking significant marriage counseling and to working on rebuilding trust. Ozzy had multiple indiscretions to the point that Sharon would say that she'd had enough, but then she seemed to have seen enough worth in her marriage to work through the problems and reconcile.* Sharon does not come across as a weak woman who is allowing her husband liberties to do whatever he wants but rather as a forgiving, and, yes, practical person who is willing to try to re-create the trust and respect that she demands in her relationship. While I am not saying that everyone must be a Sharon (or indulge the acting-out of would-be Ozzys), I just want you to consider all perspectives before taking this step.

Now you may say, "I hear all of this, but I am still done with him." You considered the answers to the questions I just provided and were honest as you evaluated your marriage. You considered your history and experience as a couple and did not sugarcoat anything. You analyzed this information and formed the conclusion—that, yes, divorce is the

---

*Or, the skeptic in me may say, that it was easier to forgive Ozzy when she saw the checks rolling in from her reality TV show about their marriage.

way to go. So now it is necessary to think about a different set of questions that could dictate the course of your future. Here are further questions to ask yourself:

- Will you be accepting about not seeing your children every day? Remember, even in the most conservative of custody agreements, there are going to be times when your kids are with their father (remember Evan and Matthew from chapter 1?) This could be difficult for you, especially if you have been the primary caregiver or a full-time mom.

- Are you ready to be a single parent when your children are with you? Sure, you feel like your spouse does nothing to help out anyway, but if you need to run to the store for something, he is a living, breathing adult who can stay in the home when the baby is sleeping. Once he is no longer in the picture, you need to wake that baby up to go to the store.

- What type of housing situation do you realistically envision? How do you think your children will react to going back and forth between two households? How flexible do you think you and your spouse can and will be once you are divorced?

- What lifestyle changes are you willing to make? Remember, divorce creates expense to all involved parties—not income—and it is more expensive to run two households than one. If your financial situation is tight right now, it is probably going to be tighter post-marriage, no matter how much financial support you believe you might receive.

- Are you willing to forego luxuries in lieu of necessities? Can you deal with the idea of skipping vacations? What about your kids' activities? How will new financial restraints affect them?

- What material possessions in your current life are you willing to do without? Remember, there is no set standard with regard to who gets what in a divorce. While you might believe you are entitled to the house or 50 percent or more of your combined assets, the legal system might feel differently.

DIVORCE IS NOT THE TANGO—IT DOES NOT TAKE TWO

Now, even if you decided that you are not sure you are ready to divorce, ready or not—it may happen anyway because your spouse may be. Common divorce "tells" that I am about to identify for you have usually already escalated by the time a potential client shows up at my office. And yes, some clients have had the rug pulled out from under them—they are in shock and feel totally blindsided. But marriages rarely go from "till death do us part" to "I cannot even stand to breathe the same air as you" overnight. There are always red flags, and usually, they take time to unfurl. And yet, at the same time, you may not want to see the signs—even when the writing is clearly on the wall. Denial is understandable—the ending of a marriage—*your* marriage—is heartbreaking. But you need to work to get past that—and the goal is to be alert and look for behavior changes that may show whether a potential split is on a soon-to-be ex-spouse's mind.

- <u>Your partner's communication style does a total 180.</u> It is one thing to have a day where your spouse simply does not feel like talking, but it is another entirely when your husband decides to shut down. He completely stops filling you in on what is happening in his life, and you effectively become a bystander watching from outside of what was once a life you shared. If you suddenly feel like the person sharing your home is an empty shell of his former self (or even more telling: if he has actually *stopped* complaining—be careful what you wish for), there is a good chance he is thinking about how to get out of the marriage. Shutting down the lines of communication and distancing oneself is just one way people make themselves care less about their relationships—making it easier to pull the plug when they deem the time is right.

- <u>Financial behavior and conversations about cash begin to morph.</u> This isn't just about financial secrets in a relationship—though that is certainly a tell—it could also include a suddenly generous spouse plying you with gifts or trips out of the blue, to distract and placate you. It could be that there are new bank accounts and old passwords that are unexpectedly being changed. Financial changes within a relationship can often signal that your partner is starting to think about the future—and what it looks like without you in it. Be aware of gripes about changes in earning potential, a reduction in compensation or bonuses, or other "I'm so poor" complaints—especially if your spouse has had a solid career history and job performance. It could be a setup to reduce financial expectations and responsibilities when he says, "I want a divorce."

- <u>They are annoyed about *everything*.</u> Look, every married person can annoy their partner. However, committed spouses usually get over it. But if your partner is suddenly always on edge, and you are not able to smooth the tension with a hug, kiss, or through whatever other "magic" you have used in the past, you may not be imagining things. The arm that jerks away from your touch, the snort or eye roll at something you say, the testy snap over nothing—these may all be signs that he is checking out of the relationship and thinking about how to cut the cord. His feelings of annoyance may not necessarily be about you—

but rather relate to his confusion regarding how to present his change of heart.

- <u>Your spouse has taken a great interest in other things—except you.</u> Any long-term relationship is always going to have its ebbs and flows. There are going to be times when both of you are interested in a new hobby or venture, and other times where one of you might have just discovered a new passion. There will be some nights when you watch TV sitting on the couch together, and other times when you are upstairs and he is downstairs. (Why watch football highlights when you just spent the last two hours watching the game?) That is completely normal. What is *not* normal is when one partner seemingly has moved on to finding a new singular interest in hanging out with friends, traveling solo, and fun new hobbies that do not involve you—and hasn't even *tried* to include you. Disinterest creates distance—emotionally and physically. If you feel like you have been pushed out of the fun activities or the other events you used to share together—and pretty much all the way off your spouse's calendar—it could very well portend that the end of the marriage is near.

- <u>Could he be cheating?</u> If your spouse is suddenly possessive of electronic devices, is abruptly required to work late or go on "business trips," has started working out and dressing sharp, or is even overcompensating when it comes to your relationship, pay attention. I am sorry to say that cheating can happen, and it can be an awful and blindsiding betrayal. Many marriages can survive infidelity—it can even bring couples closer by airing out their issues and forcing a course-correction and recommitment. But if any of the aforementioned things are happening—especially combined with the first four points on this list—then your spouse could be getting ready to serve you with divorce papers.

- <u>Everything is totally fine and boring; nothing to see here.</u> <u>Right?</u> I once had a client—let's call her Lucy—who was divorcing her charming, attractive husband who was a doting father to their children and treated her with love and respect. They got along great, had a lovely life, it all seemed like happily ever after. But somewhere along the line Lucy had had a three-year affair with a handsome young painter. Her husband never found out about the affair—he had never even sensed something was amiss with his wife or noticed her growingly distant feelings. Life went on—because why fix what does not seem broken—and then (to his shock) she asked for a divorce. Said Lucy: "I had an affair for three years and I barely hid it. But he still never noticed." Lucy realized she had become invisible to him due to the normalcy of their relationship. Having someone notice you—and connect with you—is an intangible but essential need in a relationship. People really do get lulled by normalcy—on both sides. One side uses it as camouflage for avoidance, and the other side gets blindsided. Usually in retrospect it becomes clear when things started to change, but habit is powerful—and there's nothing that disguises distance in a marriage better than a pleasant, orderly life. This is hardly a red flag to keep an eye out for—the very point of it is that it doesn't wave! But it's worth pointing out that sometimes both parties can be sharing a perfectly nice marriage in which they actually each feel very much alone.

As you read this list, you may have been thinking, *Holy shit! I bought this book as a "just in case," but now I am really nervous!* I do not want to scare you—that is truly not my intent. However, I do want you to open your eyes. With that being said, there could be other reasons why your husband is exhibiting odd behavior. Just because your spouse may be doing something on this list does not automatically mean your marriage is over. There are always going to be ups and downs in any relationship. This is human nature and especially true when you are simultaneously acting as a couple as well as independently operating beings, capable of changing and evolving the older you grow. For instance, when you are in the middle of raising your kids, it is not always going to be time for sexy lingerie and champagne but instead may be quickies in the morning before the batteries on the kids' phones die. But do not be naive either. It is always a wise strategy to take off the blinders to try to figure out what is going on so you are not shocked when divorce papers suddenly turn up on your kitchen table.

IS THIS THE RIGHT TIME TO GET DIVORCED?

So you now know you are ready to get divorced (and/or your spouse is) but now the timing of said divorce is the question. The right time is not always yesterday, but it could be tomorrow. Or you may feel like "No time like the present!"—but timing can be key, so you need to be strategically smart about when you pull the divorce trigger. Here are some reasons why it might make more sense to live in a marriage that is far from perfect for a little while longer:

- Your husband owns a business that is on the verge of great success (think MacKenzie Bezos—what would have happened if she pulled the plug years ago?). If you start divorce proceedings now, you may not get a piece of that increased value, despite the fact you were present and gave your blood, sweat, and tears during the painstaking endeavor.

- Your children are babies and in what could be called the "danger stage." They are unable to communicate and you have concerns about your husband's ability to properly care for your little ones.

Many parents feel better about their ex being left alone with the children when the kids are able to adequately communicate their needs.

- Your children are older and about to leave for college, and you want to stick it out for one or two more years until they are on their own. This way you do not have to fight about custody and your children will not have to live with you through the divorce process.

- Your husband is paying all the bills, you are living a nice lifestyle, and you do not want that to end. There is nothing wrong with being honest and recognizing that while you know your marriage is dead, it still serves the purpose of allowing you and your children to have an Instagram-ready life. If you want to continue this, either wait for him to decide to end the marriage or wait until you feel the financial comfort is no longer worth it.

- You are in school or just started a new job and you want to feel confident about your own finances before you throw away the security blanket.

- You need more time to get your financial affairs in order, learn what marital assets exist, track your expenses, put away a little cash for security, and open credit cards to increase your access to funds.

It could also be the perfect time to file for divorce for any of the following reasons:

- You own a business that is on the verge of great success. If you start divorce proceedings now, your husband may not get a piece of that increased value (remember Blake and her jewelry business?). If entrepreneurs Jennifer Hyman and Jennifer Fleiss, two friends from

Harvard Business school and the cofounders of Rent the Runway, an online service that provides designer dress and accessory rentals, decided they wanted to divorce their husbands (I am not even sure of their marital status, but using them as examples) but felt like they did not have the energy to do it when the company was a pie-in-the-sky idea, they would have greatly regretted it now since their company was recently valued at one billion dollars.

- You have the type of job that is more bonus-heavy than base-heavy and you are due to receive a large bonus at the end of the year. You want to file a summons right away (assuming your spouse is not also bonus-heavy, with larger bonuses than you) because every day you don't, 1/365th of your bonus is being deposited into the marital pot. Even if you are not bonus-heavy but outearn your spouse, you may want to consider filing sooner than later.

- You fear that your spouse may be losing his job or his income is about to take a great dip.

- Your children are older and about to leave for college, and (depending on the state you live in) you may only receive child support until your child goes to college. If you want to be a recipient of child support (and want to enjoy it with your spouse not in the house), you may want to file now.

- Your children are young and aligned more with you, so you would have increased odds of having more parenting time (at least for now, until your daughter hits her teenage years and she turns on you and could tell a judge that she wants to live with her father because he lets her watch R-rated movies).

- Your spouse fears court. Plus, he hates the idea of paying your legal fees, so it may be a strategic move to file because it will make him want to settle quicker if he thinks you may run to court (but be sure that this move does not financially work against you for the reasons previously listed).

Generally speaking, the higher-earning spouse wants to file for divorce when the stock market is down and the income levels are down because there is less to distribute and support packages can be lower. In the same vein, the lower-earning spouse wants to file when the stock market is high and the income levels are higher because there is more to distribute and support packages could be higher. (This is why I joke that divorce attorneys—and funeral directors—always have job protection in any economy.)

I can't tell you what to do here—you alone know how you feel about your marriage and whether you wish to remain in it. But however you may feel, I urge you to take a moment to consider these factors with a clear head and a jaundiced eye, and really think about your financial status and basic needs. Like I said, divorce isn't the tango. You are dancing alone here, so listen to the music and move accordingly.

STEPS TO TAKE BEFORE YOU PULL ANY TRIGGER

Your emotions may tell you that once you've decided you want to move forward with divorce, you want to sit your spouse down and tell him the news. My advice is to resist that urge until you have your ducks in a proverbial row. Here are some to-dos that I would recommend once you have decided that the time is now:

- Try to figure out your financial picture. While I understand that finances may not represent your "happy place," you want to obtain as much financial information as possible now. If there are bank statements sitting out on the kitchen table, take note of the

balances and the account numbers (snap a picture if that is easier). If you have access to the tax returns, make copies of them.
If you have that thick book with all the colorful tabs that your
financial adviser hands you every year that lists all your financial
assets (the one you normally throw out right after the annual
meeting), put it in a safe place for now. Try to recall conversations that your spouse had with you about his bonuses or deferred compensation accounts (I know it all sounded like "blah
blah blah" before). It would not be the worst thing for you to ask
your spouse about the details of his income at dinner as long as it
would not seem too out of the norm. Be a financial detective. If
you are not working—it may be a good time to speak to a head-
hunter to get a sense of what your earning potential could be. Pay
attention to your spending—especially cash expenditures. Your
attorney will ask you to ultimately fill out a form where you will
need to list all your expenses—so may as well start preparing for
that now.

- <u>Start keeping a diary of child-related events.</u> Note which ones
  he attends and those he does not attend. Hopefully you will never
  need this information, but if there is a custody fight in your future,
  you may not recall details when being questioned by your attorney. But please be careful where you keep said diary. On that note,
  you may want to open a separate email account for just divorce-
  related emails. If that is too much trouble, then if you have a family
  member or friend you trust, you can send important notes to that
  person and then erase the emails from your email account (and be
  sure to empty your deleted file as well).

- <u>Get liquid.</u> Again, I hope that it does not come to this, but if you
  are financially dependent on your spouse and do not have liquid
  assets in your own name (or in joint name), you could be vulner-

able. It is a seemingly juvenile move, but there is the possibility of your spouse "cutting you off" and you need to be prepared for this assertion of control once he learns you are looking to divorce. Yes, your attorney can make an immediate motion to the court to prevent this, but the reality is that courts do not move quickly. Start opening credit cards, and if you can get ones that provide cash advances, all the better (it is also important to establish a credit score if you do not have one because you always just used your spouse's cards). If possible, you may want to start storing some money in a sock draw (or a Jimmy Choo boot). I would not suggest you make large withdrawals from a bank account (unless that is your normal habit), but having some cash on hand in case he makes a dick move is smart.

- <u>Consider a little shopping.</u> Now, I would love to advise you that you should throw caution to the wind and buy that Hermès bag you have been eyeing (that advice would make everyone want to buy this book). I am not going that far, but I would say that if you are about to get divorced and/or start an action for divorce, your access to money is going to be monitored in a way that it may not have been during the marriage. So, depending on your financial situation (do not put yourself further in to debt for this), if you have been putting off a big purchase (for either you or the kids) that you know your spouse would veto, you may want to consider doing it now—before the financial plug is pulled.

- <u>Call an attorney and have an initial consultation.</u> The best decisions are the most educated decisions. In order for you to be in the best position to have a fruitful discussion with your spouse, you need to be aware of what process you want to use for the divorce and where your strengths and weaknesses in your case lie. I discuss this more in the next chapter, which I suggest you read before calling an attorney and definitely before saying anything about your intentions to your spouse.

Ultimately, I simply want to make sure you are jumping into this potential divorce with your eyes wide open and while wrapped in a firm sense of reality. Think hard about what your post-marriage life and world will look like, because it could make you realize that maybe you and your husband can work it out—together. Or engaging in this exercise could prove the opposite—that you are making the right decision and you are ready to move forward with your divorce.

You Need to Put on Your Own Oxygen Mask First—Self-Care Is Key

When I'm tired, I rest. I say,
"I can't be superwoman today."
—JADA PINKETT SMITH

Forgive me for the Captain Obvious statement but "Divorce is really fucking hard." It can feel like it is killing you from the inside out. You can't sleep, you can't eat (interesting diet plan—you did want to lose those last five pounds), and you probably will ask people to repeat their questions a million times because your focus is elsewhere. It is supposed to be hard. Reese Witherspoon once said (when speaking of her divorce from Ryan Phillippe): "By the way, if it's not painful, maybe it wasn't the right decision to marry to begin with. Those are the appropriate emotions."[1] So we can agree that these emotions are normal, and we can also agree that they suck.

This is why it is so important to take care of yourself when going through this process. You will feel like your needs are low on the list of priorities when you are trying to keep your children balanced, buttering up your ex, and providing financial documents to your attorney. But your needs cannot be placed at the bottom of the pile, because if you are a sleep-deprived, malnourished mess whose head is floating somewhere above your body, then you will not be able to take care of everyone else's needs and nobody wins.

WHO AM I NOW? WHAT TO
DO WITH IDENTITY ISSUES

In order to be in the best position to take care of yourself, you need to understand exactly what is wrong. Common sense would say, "I am getting divorced, my kids are only with me 50 percent of the time, and my net worth was cut in half—that's what is fucking wrong!" Yeah, I get that—but it is actually more than even what appears on the surface. Again, I am not trying to play shrink here—but in my years of experience dealing with the emotions of my divorcing clients, I find that many of my clients go through a personal identity crisis that is often overlooked or undervalued (unless you have a good therapist). Think about it. From the day you were born, you were somebody's daughter. Then you became someone's friend and girlfriend, and finally, someone's wife. After that, you may have emerged as someone's mother. Your identity has primarily been connected to your relationship with another person. So, what happens when that connection is broken and how does this affect your identity? The key to getting through this identity turmoil is to recognize it and then take steps to create a new identity—one that will withstand changes in a relationship status.

THE MANY FACETS OF DIVORCE

There at least are four different areas of one's identity that can be affected by divorce. They are legal, financial, parental, and social. Let me explain the nuances of each.

The legal divorce

When most people think of divorce, their thoughts immediately turn to the legal divorce; the fact that the state no longer considers you and your ex a married couple. This is the part of the divorce that often involves lawyers and requires a judge to rubber-stamp your paperwork and declare you "officially divorced." Many view this as the easiest part of the divorce because it is ministerial in nature.

While the legal divorce comprises paperwork and a rubber stamp, there is an identity shift that occurs when you receive the judgment back from the court. You are no longer a "wife" (unless you become one in the future). You check a new box when asked if you are "married" or "single." You file your taxes differently. No longer do you qualify for the $500K capital-gains tax exemption when selling a house. Ultimately, there are many legal ramifications to being legally divorced.

The financial divorce

The financial divorce is considered the meat and potatoes of the divorce. This process involves dissolving the financial unit of your marriage, identifies the specifics of how the assets and liabilities will be divided, and establishes support structures. Again, as you know, this is often handled by attorneys and financial advisers. You may be more involved in this stage, as it will have ramifications on your day-to-day post-divorce life. I tell my clients this is the business part of the divorce. Emotion needs to be minimized, and one must focus on the numbers (unless you are falling victim to the guilt window).

Your identity can take a hit in the financial divorce. As you know—running two households costs more than one. Depending on your financial circumstances, you may have less money to spend than you did while you were married, which can affect the way you live your life and see yourself. Ms. Generous who used to invite the neighborhood over for steak and lobster dinners might be faced with hosting backyard barbecues with burgers and hot dogs. However, at the same time, and depending on how the finances were handled during the marriage, it is possible you may have more control over money in your new post-divorce life. You might now be a financial decision maker, and this can be scary, exciting, and annoying—all at the same time. You will need to take the call with the financial adviser and pay attention to what you are spending, as it is now "your money."

Other changes could occur as well that involve your financial identity. For example, if your children go to a private school that mandates contributions, you and your ex may each get separate calls soliciting donations, as you are now individual households. There may also be separate birthday celebrations for the children (although I recommend combining these occasions for emotional and financial reasons) and other activities that cost more than they did before.

However, obtaining the financial divorce may be one of the most compelling reasons to pursue a divorce because it separates you from his debt. No longer will he be able to use your hard-earned money to buy unnecessary sports memorabilia (how many sports bobbleheads does one man need anyway?).

The parental divorce

The parental identity crisis is one of the hardest identity shifts to deal with, as I will discuss more later. It is often one of the most emotionally charged areas of divorce. This identity deals with how you co-parent with someone who is no longer in your home and is outside of your control. The idea that you are not the only person who gets the calls when Jenny is sick or having your ex sign permission slips—it can make you question who you thought you were.

The social divorce

The social divorce is probably one of the parts of divorce that receives the least attention—but it is meaningful and has a huge impact on your social identity. This is where your friends choose a side (even though they may pretend they don't) and you may need to find new single friends to socialize with. I think of the HBO show *Curb Your Enthusiasm*, starring Larry David, specifically, the episode after Larry and Cheryl broke up.

One of their mutual friends comes to see Larry to talk to him about a party he is throwing. The man basically tells Larry that he cannot come to the party because Cheryl was going to be there. He says, "My wife and I talked about it and we chose Cheryl." While some people may not be as blatant as that, the fact is, it happens.

There will also be the married friends who distance themselves from you because they believe that divorce is "contagious" and they do not want to catch it. It is also possible that you will face being approached by the yenta moms who are so curious to find out the specifics of your breakup (again, so they can make sure to avoid the same fate). Finally, if you are attractive or have a naturally flirtatious manner, you will also have other men (sometimes the husbands of friends) who will hit on you—which will likely sour your relationship with their wives.

During the social divorce, your identity takes a real shift (for good and bad), as you now may have to find some new friends. You are not always part of the same social circles anymore, and realizing you are not invited to events you have looked forward to in the past could be disheartening and upsetting.

To survive this, you need to make decisions early on about how you want to move forward socially. Are you comfortable spending time with your best friend and her husband even if it is at a table for three? Will you want to take this time and sow your wild oats? Think of it as changing schools when you were a child; you have the ability to determine who you want to be and how you are perceived. While the social aspects of the divorce may seem overwhelming, know that in time you will figure out what works for you and be able to navigate through this new social maze.

THE SPOUSAL IDENTITY CRISIS

A very common situation I deal with involves the full-time stay-at-home mother who is married to a Wall Street husband (please excuse the stereotypes here, but sometimes they are right on point). I have so many clients who fall victim to this identity crisis that I do not even know who to choose to speak about. One client specifically stands out because she was the quintessential story—let's call her "Liza." Liza was one of the most dedicated mothers I've ever met. She concerned herself with every possible need or want her children had. She attended every baseball practice and game, would sit quietly through every violin lesson (which you can only truly appreciate if your kid takes violin, because bad violin is like needles being stabbed in your eardrums), was president of the PTA, had made homemade baby food comprising all organic ingredients, and helped direct the school plays—all without breaking a sweat. Liza was married to an investment banker who made millions of dollars a year, and so she was in the financially advantageous position of having the means to do everything and anything for her children and took her job as mom very seriously. She was the woman other moms of lesser means loved to hate (yet she was so incredibly nice that I doubted the other moms really hated her—but they wanted to).

Now, enter the divorce proceedings, where Wall Street dad wants fifty-fifty time with the children. These are the same kids Liza had reared, practically chewing their food for them baby-bird style before depositing it into their waiting mouths. From the perspective of this overly attentive mother, there was no way this man could take care of these children whom she had done everything for. What stung even worse was that her husband would often complain that Liza was a "lady who lunched" and did nothing all day except hang out with her friends while he worked his ass off, making millions of dollars a year to afford said lunches. Liza would then retort that he had no understanding of her day-to-day life, which would earn a rude response about trading places and how Liza definitely could not go to Wall Street and make a few million a year, but he could definitely do her job and make PB&J sandwiches with the crusts cut off (which goes to show how little he knew—she would never make PB&J sandwiches for her children).

So now the nightmare that kept Liza from leaving this unappreciative and narcissistic asshole for the last few years had come true. He had access to *her* children (that was how she saw them) and was tasked with taking care of them. Sure, he was feeding them McDonald's, they were wearing mismatched clothing, and their math homework was done in crayon, but they survived the nights with him. He proved he could "take care of them," but Liza still couldn't get a job on Wall Street.

This is truly devastating to many women (including Liza), and addresses some deep fears—he was right: her job as mommy was not that hard. I can see the vision blurring with tears of all of the Lizas who are reading this book. Before those tears fall, please realize he is not right. Yes—he can spend a few bucks at McDonald's, and the children will not be picked up by child protective services for wearing different-colored socks, but what you (and Liza) do is beyond the basic.

The valuable lesson that must be learned, and part of the process of your self-care during (and after) a divorce, is how important it is for your identity to go beyond that of wife and mother (not to belittle how important those roles are). I encourage clients and friends to always have something in their lives in addition to their mommy or wife duties, whether it be a job outside the home, working with a charity, having some special social hobby, playing a sport, or whatever. Forget about divorce—if you allow your identity to be solely wrapped up in your children, what happens when they grow up? You should also have some place in your life where you can go and people know your name and do not know you only as Gia's mother or Rich's wife. You cannot connect all your identities to another person, otherwise you will be lost if that relationship is ever severed. It is imperative you have something in your life that no matter what relationship ends or changes—your name remains the same.

EACH DAY COUNTS

Part of your self-care is to be prepared to face a myriad of emotions when going through the divorce process. From sadness to anger to fear and anxiety—the emotional spectrum is broad and diverse. Therefore, the question remains: With so many conflicting and confusing emotions flooding your body twenty-four hours a day and seven days a week, how does one still succeed at work, get the kids to school, and even simply remember to brush her teeth in the morning? As much of a clichéd statement as this may appear to be, let me tell you frankly—you retain your sanity during a divorce by taking each day one at a time and taking time to make sure your needs are met.

I had a client once—let's call her Madison—who was a total emotional mess when she walked into my office. At our initial consultation, she was barely able to tell me her email address without sucking in breaths between sobs. It was a stereotypical story of her husband having an affair with a woman he commuted into work with. Madison, a stay-at-home mom, said she did not see it coming and was in total shellshock. I knew Madison needed to become emotionally sturdier before she would be ready to embark on the divorce process.

To become stronger, sometimes you need to lean into your emotions, take the time to process them, and flush them through your system so you can be ready to move past them.

After I had asked the pertinent questions I needed to ask for my initial consultation and Madison told me her story (as much as she could while choking back tears), I said to her, "Do you remember those days-of-the-week underwear that we wore as children?" I could tell she was taken aback, as she was expecting great words of wisdom to come out of my mouth, not a reminder about how annoyed she got when she lost her Tuesday Underoos. Being polite, I am sure, she admitted that she did recall the panties. I (jokingly) suggested that she see if they came in adult sizes, because I wanted her to follow this schedule:

Sad Tuesdays

On Tuesdays, I told Madison that she should spend the day feeling shitty about her situation. This was the day that she was to give herself the time to mourn the loss of her marriage, her former identity, and the images she created in her mind of what her life was going to look like. I told her that once she got her kids on the school bus, she could make it all about her and carve out some time of the day to lie under the covers and cry. Go ahead and drone on about how she could not believe this happened to her and that she was so unlucky in love and in life. She could ignore her friends and family who would say, "He was not good for you anyway! You are going to be better off!" and "He was an asshole!" (which, even if it was true, it would not be true on Tuesdays, because that was her sad day).

Mad Wednesdays

Just as she was allowed to be sad on Tuesdays, we agreed that she also needed the luxury of having a day to be mad too, and that was to happen on Wednesdays. To take some time to not rise above it all and simply get pissed. As Tuesday came to a close and she was surrounded in used Kleenex, I joked that she could use those tissues for kindle—along with her ex's autographed baseball cards—for a bonfire, as Wednesday was her day to be mad! (Please note again—I was only kidding and not advocating torching her ex's possessions—Mad Wednesdays are only for figurative bonfires.)

Another note for Mad Wednesdays is to be careful not to do anything that you may end up regretting later and try to blame it on Mad Wednesday (so *no* social media!). I told her that if she needed to write something, then the exercise I use is I write the email I want to send (but place my own email address in the "to" field) and say whatever the hell I want in this message. I usually erase the email after I have written whatever it was I *really* wanted to say rather than actually sending it to myself. However, there are times when I do hit send, because the *whoosh* sound offered by my phone provides great satisfaction. I could tell Madison liked this idea, however I warned her not to play around with placing her ex's email address in the "to" field just for shits and giggles because too often people hit send by mistake. Also, remember if you play this game and do send it to yourself, be sure to erase it the next day from your in-box (and your sent folder and deleted emails). You never want someone snooping around in your email (either your ex or your kids) and have this be discovered. Ultimately, the whole exercise is just about allowing yourself to be angry—be it rational or not.

Another warning I issued to Madison (and now to you) is to take heed on Mad Wednesdays and avoid saying too much to a friend about your allowed anger levels, because while you know that when Thursday comes you no longer have permission to be a raging lunatic bitch, your friend may not forget things that easily.

Anxiety Thursdays

Thursday was slated as the day where Madison could express all the anxiety she was feeling. This was her day to spend time worrying about things she knew would never really happen. *Will I really lose custody of the children although I have always been the primary caretaker? Will I really have to sleep on the street? Will he really get one of each of the shoes in my collection?* Obviously the answer is no, but these are worries that caused her anxiety. I told her we could have a weekly call set up so she could ask me the same questions over and over again (she liked this until she saw her legal bills—anxiety can be expensive).

*Mondays and Fridays: the days where
you get your shit together*

While she had to know I was not going to let her emotions dictate her behavior all week, I could tell Madison was not pleased when I discussed Mondays and Fridays. Mondays are the beginning of the week, and while she had the extravagance of feeling sad on Tuesday, angry on Wednesday, and anxious on Thursday, she needed to be responsible on Monday and organize herself for the week ahead. I explained that this may mean creating a strategy for herself at work (because I also advised her that she will need to be going back to work at some point—insert more sobbing) or coordinating her children's activities, but that she needed to be focused on Mondays. I also slipped in that it was imperative she get all the documents and information together that her attorneys required on Mondays, so we could work on her case during the week when she was going through her emotional days.

Mondays are like the day where one must pack for a vacation so you are organized and ready to go. I am not saying you cannot experience your emotions on Mondays, but you need to keep it in check so your life does not spiral out of control.

On the other end of the spectrum is Friday, which are like Mondays. However, in this case, you have just returned from your vacation and you need to unpack and do the laundry. It is time to get out of your emotional vacation mode and reorganize. Start getting ready for the weekend; it does not matter if that entails getting yourself or your children organized. Plans need to be made, soccer bags need to be packed, and your house needs to be clean in the event that your big date on Saturday night comes back to your house for a nightcap. (I got a big eye roll from Madison at the date comment).

Recovery weekends

I wanted to prepare Madison for Saturdays and Sundays, as they can be the most difficult days for people who are dealing with the divorce process because the routines found on weekends are broken. There are usually more social plans on the weekends, which can be good but can also be bad. Additionally, the weekends are when children often shift back and forth between homes, which can cause a lot of emotional pain or strife (in both you and the children). This is why it is so important to prepare for the emotional, as well as logistical, elements of the weekend on Friday. In the beginning, the goal of Saturday and Sunday is to just get through them so you can get back into a normalized routine on Monday. But many people really enjoy the weekends because either the children are around—or they are not! (Just wait until the last secret, about divorce being a blessing.) If you can get to a place where you can recognize the weekends offer "me" time and embrace that—then Saturday and Sunday can be party time!

At this point in the consult, Madison was amused and started looking on Amazon to see if they made these day-of-the-week undies in thongs.

LIVING YOUR LIFE—AND DEALING WITH EMOTIONS

I recognize that not everyone (including maybe Madison) has the true leisure of crawling under the covers and shedding endless tears on Sad Tuesdays, nor are you able to put off the important report due to your boss on Mad Wednesday because you are busy sending angry emails to yourself. Moreover, you cannot really afford to keep your attorney on the phone on Anxiety Thursday. So, if you do not have the time to do all that during the week, then maybe a better option is to use the weekends when you are not with your children to deal with your emotions.

Regardless of the day of the week, the point is that you need to feel the emotions you are going to experience during the divorce and not keep them pent up inside as part of the way to take care of yourself. It is necessary to be who you truly are and not wear a tough-woman facade all the time. During a divorce, it is normal to be sad—even if you are the one who initiated the split. It is also fine to be angry, and anxiety is a natural human response to stressful situations. Normal and natural reactions to this life change are going to come your way—so grant yourself permission to have them. If some of this is too hard to deal with on your own, enlist the help of a therapist, take a yoga class, learn to meditate, find solace with friends or family—anything to help you get back on track.

IGNORE THE HAIRDRESSER WITH A PhD: HOW TO DEAL WITH OTHERS' OPINIONS

As part of the self-care you need to administer during your divorce, you need to sometimes protect yourself from those who are trying to help you. The moment you tell someone you are going through a divorce is the exact moment you are suddenly being offered a diatribe of unwelcome advice about how you should now handle your life. It does not matter if you are sitting in your mother's living room with your great-aunt Beverly, whom you have not seen in twenty years, or perched across the spa from a woman sitting naked under a towel who you have never spoken to in your life—seemingly everyone who is anyone feels the need (and the privilege) to offer you advice and counsel on what is happening in your personal life. And in light of all this unsolicited feedback, you are still paying people like me—your lawyer—who actually know what the hell they are talking about (at least they should) for the real guidance and direction. Therefore, I need to warn you that listening to the peanut gallery around you presents a serious issue—and it could cost you financially, emotionally, and legally. I implore you, shut these voices out for your own good. Do not heed their advice. A well-meaning friend might be absolutely certain on one issue or another, but that does not mean she is not full of shit.

Friends don't let friends give legal advice. It is a given that you have known many of your friends and loved ones much longer than you have been acquainted with your divorce attorney. And you probably also believe that your best friend from third grade, your sister or brother, or even your parents would never steer you wrong (at least not intentionally). However, their input could actually be causing you to second-guess your decision to split with your spouse, even when you have spent the time and effort analyzing your situation and coming to the conclusion that is right for you. What is more, their input and feedback could also be presenting undue and unnecessary challenges to your case, whether you realize it or not.

Many times, when a couple is divorcing, friends and loved ones may let their personal interests cloud the advice they give. These people might complain about how your divorce could affect their lives so you even feel guilty about the burden you are putting on them—as if you do not have enough to worry about. For example, your mother may complain that if you get divorced, going on family vacations together will be that much more difficult because the adult-to-child ratio will be off. In turn, these voices can fuel new forms of negativity inside you. It can increase your stress level and make your life more difficult. Their advice can even lead you to doubt your attorney's guidance, which then can affect your case and your future. Ultimately, the noise from the people around you may not help you get through your divorce with your head in the right place or your confidence intact.

NO ONE UNDERSTANDS YOUR SITUATION THE WAY YOU DO

When a woman finds out she is pregnant or has just had a baby, she is dealing with all the stuff that mothers-to-be and new moms have to face. Everything is a novel experience for her, from the way she is feeling physically to the personal worries or concerns she is dealing with mentally, spiritually, or emotionally. She is learning how to operate and adjust to this new reality in her life. But, it is her experience—her journey.

Regardless, that does not stop everyone and anyone from offering their feedback on her life and the choices she is making. I remember when I was pregnant with my first child and in that stage where I was showing but my stomach was not hard yet (you know what I mean—you just feel fat) and some woman decided to come and comment on the type of snack I was purchasing and proceeded to rub my belly (as if I was Buddha or something!). This was while she espoused advice on how to handle my pregnancy. It is as if every woman who has gone through childbirth thinks she has a free pass to touch another woman's stomach!

The point I am trying to make here is that no matter what happens in your life, there is going to be someone who feels they know your absolute truth, that they understand exactly the course you should take and how to ultimately correct said course if you are not following their advice. And they are going to offer this wisdom whether you ask for it or not. I suggest you find the mute button and press it.

THERE ARE NO ABSOLUTES

In my life as a divorce attorney, clients regularly consult with me, not just about their cases but also their insecurities, worries, and fears. I personally find it ironic when a sister or a friend has told one of my clients "how it is" because of whatever situation she is facing. My personal favorite is when someone advises, "He cheated, and therefore your marriage is over. How will you ever trust him again?" or even the exact opposite of that, "He cheated, just give him another chance. Boys will be boys, you know? I am sure it was just a one-time thing."

Yes, the insight of others likely comes from a place of caring and concern—people do care about you and want you to have a good life. But the fact of the matter is that it is misguided and positioned from a place of almost complete ignorance. What you must realize is that there are no absolutes in divorce. There are no hard-and-fast rules that every divorce follows or subscribes to.

Every marriage has so many different layers. It is naive to think generalized or generic concepts apply to your situation. Remember, you are not being showcased on a daytime talk show—your problems are not going to end after an hour of analysis by a TV shrink, nor are they ripe for the likes of someone such as Judge Judy. While it is true that many marriages end because of a cheating spouse, realize too that other factors are usually at play. Something has eroded within the relationship, communication has broken down, and expectations have not been met. No one else is likely to be privy to these stark realities, other than you and your soon-to-be ex-spouse.

SELF-DIALOGUE CAN BE DAMAGING

It is not only the input of others that you have to watch out for. You must also remain vigilant about the way you talk to yourself—in your heart and in your head. You might need to ignore some of the things you are telling yourself and shake up your internal dialogue in order to keep your sanity in check.

Ultimately, if you have followed my earlier advice and truly analyzed the state of your marriage, you know you have made an educated decision to divorce. Therefore, you cannot let your inner worries, fears, or negativity consume you. Yes, there are going to be times when your split is weighing heavily on you. There will be times when you feel scared and alone—as well as moments when you are angry, flat-out irate and pissed off. However, if all you do is focus on the dialogue that breaks you down, weakens you, and exposes your vulnerabilities, you will not get through this situation whole. There will be no way to become a better person or find a healthy place to exist. Your negative energy, instead, will only make the divorce process worse—it will be more of a grind to your self-confidence, and your psyche will be pulverized.

There is no positive outcome from you being hard on yourself. Nothing is to be gained by beating the hell out of yourself daily. You are already down—but you do not have to be out. My advice here is that when you find yourself focusing blame on you, take a moment to recognize what is happening and then tune it out. Flip the off button on that critical voice, and make it shut the fuck up. Set new boundaries with yourself and remember to keep on *liking* yourself. No, this might not be the easiest item on your to-do list, but you need to do it. In order to get through your divorce and move on without having to manage every unresolved issue in the book, tune out that terrible voice that seems set on telling you how wrong you are, what a loser you are, as well as any other insult or degrading comment it can come up with. Simply put, that voice is wrong. You do not deserve this bad time in your life—nor is this challenge going to last forever. You *do* have a future, and you *will* move forward.

SOCIAL MEDIA CARE

No matter how you decide to look at it, divorce is, as you know, incredibly stressful. In today's technology-driven world, however, many people believe that social media is a neutral arena. It is the type of virtual environment where you can separate yourself from the drama, express yourself, and maybe get in a little venting. After all, what good is having more than a thousand "friends" online unless you can use them as a support group, right? Wrong. No matter how much you are itching to fire off a tweet, or update your Facebook status with details about your soon-to-be ex, as part of your self-care as well as legal strategy, I strongly advise against engaging in social media during the divorce process. Social media is simply a world that can make your divorce much more difficult.

Yes, it might feel awesome to bash your ex and put it on display online. You may say, "That is the best self-care I can think of!" Think again. I encourage you to put away your phone, tablet, computer, *whatever*. Sit on your hands for goodness' sake, or purchase some mittens and sew the thumbs together! Keep your social media mouth shut while you are getting divorced from the person who has ignited your ire.

This applies to everything that might be happening in your life—even if it is on the peripheral of your divorce proceedings. Found a new beau you think is ten times the man your spouse was? Keep it to yourself. Contemplating what you are going to spend your divorce settlement on? Mum's the word. Social media might give you multiple ways for broadcasting what is happening in your life, and yes, you may be encouraged to share every stray thought and feel like sharing is caring, but no one needs this information. This is especially true as it pertains to your ex, your ex's attorney, and the judge.

I had a client once—let's call her Janell—who bashed her ex on social media, calling him a "cheat," a "liar," and saying he could not be trusted. Sure enough, his boss and other business colleagues saw her posts. He was denied the promotion he was up for (which we are guessing was connected to the post), which resulted in the income he had available for support for Janell and the children to be less than expected. Was the release really worth it?

Anything the public has access to can be used against you in court. The first thing your spouse's attorney is going to do is Google you—and Google will show what you have been up to. Opposing counsel wants to know who you are, and however you showcase yourself to the world on social media, this will be the way you are presented in court. I cannot stress this enough: If you are getting a divorce, do not go on social media and post things about your spouse or your children, because chances are, it might be used as evidence against you in court.

If you are a parent in the midst of a divorce, you have others to consider too. Your divorce is not just about you; it also involves your children. The things you say online can impact them as well.

In today's world, kids often learn how to tweet before they can say their ABCs. Keeping this in mind, how would you feel if your children saw something negative or derogatory you said about their father online? Social media posts can be long-lasting, and the fact that you delete something does not mean it has been erased. Not by a long shot. Unless you want your children to read those vicious words one day and picture your sweet face scowling, hatred oozing out every pore, just say no to social media and limit the impact of your digital footprint. Do not post anything that could make anyone question you, your ethics, your judgment, your morals, or your integrity. Just do not do it.

Here are some words of advice when you feel the urge to post on social media. When you are about to type something quickly—just to get an issue off your chest that has been bothering you, or because you are excited about something you just bought or acquired—ask yourself, "Would I be comfortable sending this tweet/post in a text directly to the judge?" or "Would it be okay if my children read this?" If the answer is yes, then feel free to type away, otherwise, stop typing.

If you are going through the divorce process and you want to say bad things about your spouse, opt to have a glass of wine with a close friend you can trust and spill your guts to her. But stay off social media. I have never heard of anyone whose problems were instantly solved after they aired their dirty laundry on social media. Sometimes loose fingers are worse than loose lips.

MANAGING EXPECTATIONS

Part of your self-care is self-protection, and part of self-protection is managing your expectations of people in this world. I once told a client who was complaining about her ex and was in disbelief that he would behave in such a way that "if you are ever disappointed, it means your expectations were too high." She responded with: "That is the most depressing thing you have ever said to me." Now, I am not saying that you should be accepting D's on your child's report card to avoid being upset with him, but I am saying that the odds are that your ex (and maybe even your friends and family) may not live up to your expectations during and after divorce. You need to prepare for the worst (but hope for the best), because I would not want the disappointment you have in your marriage ending to be magnified because you are also disappointed that your sister-in-law stopped calling to check in on you. I am hopeful that the people in your life will be supportive and behave in a way that is beyond your expectations, but I have seen too many clients fall further down the emotional ladder because the people they hoped would be there were not. So as a mode of self-protection, until you are emotionally stronger when this divorce is over, lower expectations of certain people and hopefully you will be pleasantly surprised.

WELCOME TO THE DWC
(DIVORCED WOMEN'S CLUB)

As some of your friends and family may not be supporting you in the way you may need right now (often because they just don't "get it"), I recommend finding and joining the DWC. I recognize the fact that most of the people who are reading this book never believed they would suffer the reality of being labeled as someone's "ex." Divorce is a club that you never wanted to gain entry into—it is not something you aspired to. And for sure, the cost of membership is quite expensive. However, when you acknowledge you are a member, some great friendships can be made and a sound support system formed. Therefore, start looking to others who wear the same T-shirt as you now do who are going through or who have gone through what you are facing, and find comfort in realizing shared experiences.

FORMING FRIENDSHIPS THAT ASSIST IN HEALING

When I started writing this chapter, I was reminded of a time of personal struggle in my life and my desire to affiliate with people who understood what I was going through. It was a few years ago when my father passed away, and I was devastated. However, even in the face of my sadness, I had no desire to speak with my husband or any of my best friends, as well-intentioned as they might have been, about this situation. Even though all these people were there for me, there was no way they could possibly understand what I was going through. So I shut myself off to them. I wanted to talk only to someone who had been there— someone who had lost a parent.

In turn, I ended up reaching out to a friend whom I had not been in touch with for years. Her mother had died when we were quite young, and I felt propelled by the need to speak with her about her experience. When we finally did connect, I think we talked more in one afternoon than we had the entire time we had known each other. When she said, "It does get better with time," I did not want to bash her face in as I did when other people offered the same old, tired cliché. She got it and was able to speak to me from a place of knowledge, understanding, and personal experience, which was just what I needed at that time.

While it can be incredibly helpful to be comforted by those who have experienced what you are going through and ultimately survived, there is also comfort to be had in serving as the experienced party and helping those who are just entering the circle. For instance, there was a time years ago when I had a networking lunch with a woman I had never met before. When we first sat down, she started our small chat by explaining how she had not been networking actively because her father had just passed away. The moment I realized she was part of the same club I was, I ended up opening up to her as if she were my very best friend. We took mutual comfort in being able to express deep feelings about this situation, and I could see by the expression on her face how grateful she was that I could relate to her. We ended up becoming good friends (and also found ways to do business together).

NO CLICHÉS: THERE IS A
REASON FOR EVERYTHING

The point is, at this juncture in your life you may also discover a network of divorced friends—a group who has gone through what you are facing or who are in the process of getting divorced—just like you. There is nothing wrong with connecting with this network and commiserating with them. It is okay to allow yourself to have a support system that comprises divorced women.

I believe people come in and out of your life for different reasons. I used to joke that I have some lifelong friends and I have some situational friends. Situational friends are what they sound like—people you become friends with because of a particular situation or occurrence that is happening in your life. If you are a mom, you may have "mommy friends" who are women you hang out with simply because your children are friends; you end up talking at the same birthday parties or softball games. Then, you may have "work friends," people you are friends with because you head to the same office each day. If you happened to work somewhere else, you may not retain the friendships. Of course, there are "going-out friends"—the people with whom the only thing you might have in common is that you like to go to the same places for fun. That is enough to secure the friendship. Still yet, you may even have a "very good-looking special friend" you only go to movies with because there is no talking involved, but he makes you feel good about yourself.

The point I am getting at is you may find yourself having "divorced friends," where the common thread is that you are divorced (or divorcing) and therefore are going through the same process. There is nothing wrong with having friends who move in and out of your life at certain times and serve certain purposes. Allow yourself to have the support system of other divorced women. Seek out these people because divorce is a raw and personal experience. Many times you will describe it to someone else who is not familiar, and they may never truly understand. However, divorced (or divorcing) women will be less likely to get annoyed when you are trashing your ex for the umpteenth time, or when you are speaking legalese to repeat what your divorce attorney explained to you. With this group, you will benefit and find comfort in their support and friendship—you all will speak the same language.

A TRUE SISTERHOOD

Divorced women talk to other divorced women. This makes sense, because you want to speak to people who have firsthand experience and knowledge of what you went through. While everyone will have different stories and varied experiences—some will have loved their divorce attorneys and others will have hated them. Some may have had a judge who favored their side, and others will vent about how there is no justice. Many went through mediation, and some dealt in collaborative law. Others worked it out at the kitchen table. The point here is that while no two situations will be exactly alike, there will be similar themes present in your stories.

No matter the situation, they all had to take off that wedding band. They all had to face having that dreaded conversation with their children and families. Many had to re-create and reimagine their lives and identities—and even more had to spend nights alone and decide if they liked it or not. Their situations vary—but there is a common thread. They can help you.

However, I must also offer a warning in that you must be careful about who you let into your DWC. Divorce, like death, has many stages: shock, sorrow, denial, grief, anger, and acceptance. If you have moved on to acceptance, be wary about letting someone into your circle who is deeply embedded in the anger stage. While you can be there for her and try to help her make progress to the next stage, do not let her drag you down to join her in her rage. Some people stay angry (or sad) for a very long time. Other women swear off dating men, and many hate everyone who has a penis.

Do not allow yourself to be poisoned by those who cannot move past anger or sadness. It is definitely okay to be angry and sad— it is totally normal and you should be (but only on Tuesdays and Wednesdays—joking). And I would not tell you that this other woman should be rushed through her stages either, but I do not want you to get pulled back when you are working with her to move forward. You must work to make progress in your personal journey while remaining empathetic to the situations of others. *Understand* her situation, but do not personally allow yourself to *feel* it.

From a professional perspective, I feel that getting a good support system in place alongside licensed psychological help is a perfect mix. Working with a therapist can help you better express some of the deeper issues in your closet without having to dump really personal information on people you see at your kid's baseball game. Of course, if you have a friend who has gone through a divorce, who possesses a PhD in mental health, and with whom you feel comfortable telling your deepest and darkest secrets, then by all means—you have hit the jackpot. However, if you do not have this trifecta in someone you trust, you may want to consider paying for a therapist while benefitting from a close circle of friends.

Bottom line: do what you need to do to take care of you, because if you don't take care of yourself, no one else will.

You Are Not Divorcing the Same Person You Married

Never marry a man you
wouldn't want to be divorced from.
—NORA EPHRON

Divorce law, as a practice, is very different from other areas of the law. It is more about psychological strategy, as opposed to actual statutes and the analysis of case law. While the law plays a role, it can be a pretty minor one; as in many cases the basic laws do not apply, and since 95 percent of cases settle anyway, the art of negotiation is more significant than the rule of law. When going through this process you need to take an analytical perspective and remain deliberate in your actions at all times.

I liken divorce negotiations to a game of psychological chess. You need to obtain a thorough understanding of the opposition's psyche and perspective to anticipate his next move and how he will interpret and react to what you do. If you move your pawn will he mirror your move or will he be more likely to start with an aggressive opening to threaten your king and immediately put you on the defensive? Or maybe he will be one to distract with moving his knight only to have you focus over there while he moves in to steal your queen. Whether you play chess or not, you need to have a clear understanding of the game and who is playing it. Carefully considering word choice, working to anticipate your opposition's response or reaction, and presenting options strategically are the game pieces to achieving success. Taking a calm and measured approach—much as you would in a game of chess—will help you through negotiations, aid in achieving your goals, and, ultimately, allow your soon-to-be ex to believe it was all his idea. A divorcing spouse must forgo ego and recognize that "winning" is about getting what *you* want, not keeping your ex from getting what *he* wants.

WHAT SIZE SHOE DOES HE WEAR?

When entering any negotiation, it is necessary to put yourself into the shoes of the opposing party in an effort to try to understand his concerns. This is the only way to figure out how to address these concerns and meet as many of them as possible without giving up anything important to you. And then, possibly, you can counter them. I think back to a mediation I did once where the couple—let's call them Jack and Diane—were fighting about custody of their two daughters. Jack was insistent that he wanted fifty-fifty parenting time, and Diane was refusing to agree, as she had been a stay-at-home mom since the day the first child was born and believed the kids should primarily reside with her.

Let's first hear from Jack (I am paraphrasing here):

I love my children. I work hard every day so I can provide for them. While it saddens me that they are often asleep when I leave for work in the morning and in bed when I get home at night, I try my best to spend time with them on weekends (when I am not giving myself a few hours to watch the game, because I also need some downtime). I know my wife has always dealt with the diapers, school stuff, medical stuff, and all the other kid-related stuff because she was home and available to do all that—I was out making money! Now, she wants to divorce me because she had an affair and claims it was because I was never home (which again, was because I was off making money for our family). So, because she was bored, she is taking my kids away from me and I get sparing visitation time with them. Or alternatively, she says I can see them on weekdays for dinner, but of course she knows I cannot get out of work early enough to have a five o'clock dinner (not to mention the kids will be stressed because they have after-school activities and homework). Thinking into the future, I see myself paying so much in spousal and child support that I now need to work extra hard to make enough money. The only way I see myself being able to have a normal relationship with my children is to have them sleep at my house 50 percent of the time. I will have an au pair live with me so she can be with them until I get home, I will hire Betty Crocker to do the cooking, and I will hire Alice the housekeeper to keep the house clean, and then there was a really cute interior designer I met at a cocktail party that can make my new house cozy for the kids. Problem solved on my end.

Now from Diane:

Are you fucking kidding me? I have dedicated my entire life to my husband and our children. I wake up every morning to make sure that everyone's stomach is full and school backpacks are organized and ready for the day. I know my husband belittles what I do all day—but he is clueless. He believes that toilet paper grows on the roll and that there is a supermarket fairy who magically places all his favorite foods directly in our refrigerator. He does not understand all the time-consuming minutiae that envelop my whole day as I work to make sure that everything runs smoothly for him and our children. Whether it is making sure Ashley has a white blouse and a black skirt for her clarinet concert or Jessy has the cool soccer cleats that all the other girls have (and despite the fact that they were sold out in three stores as I ran around town looking for them!), I get everything done. Yes, he scoffs at the time I spend decorating our home so that it looks a certain way, even though I am working within the budget he provides me. He says, "You do not know the value of money because you believe the ATM prints the cash you spend." However, he is more than happy to invite his friends over and take the compliments when they tell him how beautiful our home is. He does not appreciate that the dog needs to be walked three times a day because otherwise he shits on the carpet (and guess whose fault that is?). And then, this all must be done before I have to pick up the kids from school—and get one kid uptown while the other has to be downtown, both at the same time. Then there is homework time, tests that need to be studied for, sibling fights that need to be broken up, slime that needs to be cleaned off the kitchen table, and showers need to be had. All this must be done by the time Jack returns home at 8:00 p.m. But what does it matter? He walks in and throws off the bedtime schedule, riling the kids up right before they need to go to sleep because he has not seen them all day. Yes, he uses the excuse, "But I just got home, and I want to spend some time with my kids." However, he is not the one who has to deal with the monsters they are going to be in the morning when they do not get enough sleep. And why should a hot twenty-year-old Swedish au pair take care of my children when I am sitting at home willing and able to do so? There is no way Jack will be home early enough to check homework or help them study for spelling tests. And even if he was home, he would be sitting on the couch, smelling up the room, watching football. He barely even knows these kids. And, of course, it is easy for him to blame work for our failed marriage—but he also neglected to mention that he seemed to spend a lot of time with his associate. . . . (Insert breath.)*

---

*I will note that this rant is not really necessary to make the point I am making in this chapter, but I add it in to show you that I do understand the counterarguments. (I have kids too.)

As the mediator, I am a neutral party in this. However, what I wanted to do is try to get both parties to understand what was really going on here. I looked at Diane and wanted to zap my thoughts into her head so she would be strategically smart when having this discussion with Jack. She needed to understand that Jack's request was not really about having his children with him half the time. It was more than that. Diane needed to understand that Jack felt he was being severely punished for all the sacrifices he felt he made to take care of his family. He felt wronged and scared and was lashing out because he believed Diane was trying to take his children away from him.

When I am representing the Dianes of the world (and for the purposes of this paragraph, I will assume you fall in this category), I try to get clients to figure out how to assuage their husbands' fears while still maintaining their ground. It is okay to feed into the image the Jacks have of themselves as good fathers—regardless of whether this is true. As a Diane, there is no reason (beyond your own sense of vengeance) to dispel Jack of this myth. The more you insist that your version of the story is true, the more he will resist and the less progress you will make. As I am sure you would agree, being a good parent is a huge identity issue for all of us. While it takes a lot to insult me (as you can imagine, in my line of work you need thick skin), but if someone called me a "bad parent," I admit it would hurt. So instead of taking shots at your husband by reminding him he was nowhere to be seen all the nights you were up with a crying baby, assure him that you understand and appreciate the crucial role a father plays in the life of his children. And that it is very important to you that he and the children have a strong relationship and you will do all you can to facilitate that bond. You need to actually say these words (as painful as it may be) because (a) they are true, and (b) because they will help you get to an agreement you can live with.

Moreover, you need to also hear the subliminal message he is sending—he is feeling tricked and unappreciated. While I know this may nauseate you, appreciate him; when it comes down to it, he did go out and earn the money so you could stay home and have the joy of raising your children. Even if you also worked and contributed to the family income, he did as well. I promise it will not actually kill you to say to him that you understand why he feels like he is being screwed. Tell him you know he was away from home because he was working to support your family (skip over the quip about the associate). You might even consider thanking him for allowing you the opportunity to be so heavily involved in your children's upbringing (okay, maybe now I am pushing it—this is your judgment call). Ultimately, you get my point. If you are able to address his inner concerns (even if he is too emotionally stunted to see them himself), your actions could benefit you. A former client called it "bombing him with butter"—laying the smooth, creamy flattery on thick to grease him through to where you want him. If that image is kind of gross, fine, but the point is, it will get you where you need to be, with a lot less friction.*

At the end of the day, everyone wants to feel understood and appreciated. I know I am asking you to understand and appreciate him, and you may be asking, "Well, why can't he also understand and appreciate me?" I am not saying he won't—but I am saying that you need to not let this be a quid pro quo, because then you may be at a standstill, which does not help anyone. You can only control your own actions, so control them and do what you need to do to move forward—even if that means you do not get the thank-you card at the end of the day (Hallmark does not make a card that could have enough sweet sayings to truly appreciate all you do anyway). But you should still buy one for him.

---

*I give this same advice to my male clients as well.

IT IS NOT ALWAYS WHAT YOU SAY,
BUT HOW YOU SAY IT

During these conversations, which are meant to calm your ex (and that you will probably require self-medication to engage in), you need to be aware of the words you choose to use and conscious of your delivery. Focus on using neutral words—such as "parenting time" versus "visitation." Be careful not to refer to the children as "your" children (even if you do feel like they are really "your" children) but rather "our" children. Additionally, avoid using accusatory language or placing blame. Instead, keep it neutral and even say the word "we" to show you acknowledge your role in creating this mess. Try to avoid the use of many "I" words that show you are dictating or being condescending. For instance, "I think Hailey should go to bed at nine o'clock," can be switched to, "It may be beneficial for Hailey to go to bed at nine so she gets enough sleep so as not to be a monster. What do you think?" Make the kid category neutral—a place where everyone agrees that the kid's happiness is a shared goal.

Here are some additional tricks of the trade:

- Try not to attack what your ex says or get pulled into arguments with him. Show respect for his point of view and indicate your awareness that he has a different view and a right to have that different view.

- Ask for permission to have a difficult conversation. Rather than bombarding him the second he walks in the door with the demand of "We need to talk," wait until the time is right. Then, when you are both sitting at the table after dinner and the kids are off playing with their phones, say to him, "I would like to have a difficult conversation with you. Is that okay? And if so, is this a good time?"

- Do not make any absolute statements. Never say "never" and never say "always." Using those words is the easiest way to be discredited in a conversation. For instance, if you say, "I always changed the diapers," he can point to the time that your daughter's diaper was changed in the hospital when she was a newborn by a nurse and now your words hold less weight.

- Do not back him into a corner with flat rejections. For example, when you are speaking with him and he is throwing a tantrum claiming, "I will get sole custody, you will never see the children, and you will sleep on the street." Do not go back to him with "If one of us is never going to see these children again it will be you! And you will sleep on the street with all your whores!" Instead, deliver a response something to the effect of "I guess that is an option, although I see it to be unlikely. But you never know." Deflate his sails. He wants to push your buttons and goad you into pushing back. However, remember, if someone pulls your pigtails and you do not scream and cry, then there is no fun in pulling them again.

As a divorce attorney, I often joke to clients that I am their most expensive shrink. Frequently, more time is spent with clients discussing strategy and what to say and how to say it than discussing the law or casework. It is not uncommon for me to role-play with my clients (out of the gutter, please) so I can coach them on how to have difficult or challenging conversations with their spouses without losing their cool or throwing their constructive approach out the window. Ultimately, you should remain optimistic throughout your divorce that you and your soon-to-be ex will learn to communicate effectively. I am not saying you two will be chatting like old friends tomorrow. But remember everyone is raw and scared during a divorce. As such, this can be the opportune time for you and your spouse to relearn how to speak to each other so your post-divorce life is not completely miserable. It can only help you and your children in the long run.

How you say things is important, but what you write him can be even more important.

Ten Rules for Emailing with Your Ex During (and Even After) Divorce

1. Try to limit the topics to no more than three issues in an email. I find people do not tend to read or retain more than three points at a time.

2. Number the points and separate each point by a space. If you number the points, you increase the odds of all three questions being answered, and spacing makes it seem less overwhelming than a huge ranting paragraph.

3. Try to phrase your questions so answers of yes or no are possible. If you can get back a simple yes or no, you increase the odds of your questions being answered.

4. Keep the three points short. If it takes someone more than one thumb swipe on their phone to read the whole email, the odds drop that your full email will be read.

5. Try to use email for issues that do not need an immediate response. Use the phone for emergencies and figure email should have a window of twenty-four to seventy-two hours for response.

6. Try to use neutral words because you need to assume that the written word will be taken in the worst tone possible.

7. Don't cc other people on the emails and suck them into your drama. That gives the response a bigger audience and will cause

more reaction. (You can just forward it to your sister to read after you send it instead.)

8. Try to write your emails at times of the day when you know he/she will read them. If you know your ex has a manager's meeting every Tuesday at 8:30 a.m., do not write your emails during that time.

9. Do not write an explosive email while he is spending parenting time with the kids.

10. Try to end all emails on a positive note—even if you don't mean it.

WALK SOFTLY BUT CARRY A BIG STICK

Once you have learned how to address his concerns and speak (and write) to him in an effective and neutral manner, now is the time for you to gently learn how to present the facts in a way that he can hear them. This will lead to the two of you finding common ground. Possessing this skill will enable you to achieve your goals while making him believe it was his idea. For example, when dealing with the custody scenario mentioned previously, what would be the common ground that Jack and Diane share? Open the conversation with the fact they both want what is going to be best for their children and do not want this divorce to screw them up. Now, they may not share the same ideas of what is best for their kids, or maybe they do. Jack's goals might be for them to have a strong and healthy relationship with their father and for him to not feel screwed. Diane's goals also focus on their children being strong and healthy, and (whether she wants to admit it or not) she probably does want them to have a good relationship with their dad—just not 50 percent of the time. My guess is that once he is comforted knowing he will still be their father, his focus on the fifty-fifty parenting time will lessen. I am sure if he really thought about it, he would realize that having a twenty-year-old au pair is not the best person to supervise their children when he is unavailable. Therefore, Diane must communicate this in such a way where this becomes evident to him. Consider offering this question: "What schedule do you think would work best for you and for the children?" When I see this conversation take place between two parents who are both secure in the fact their children will have access to both of them and neither will be belittled, the outcome is much more productive than when one parent is fearful. If Diane can get Jack to come up with a schedule that permits the children to be with her on nights he is unavailable but still allows for flexibility (and maybe Diane gives Jack a few free weekends to play with), then he feels he is being a good dad. He has come up with a schedule that works for everyone (because let's face it, he is not going to be able to get out of work early, and having a hot au pair is like being a kid in a candy store with a sugar allergy), and his sense of control and ego are satiated as he feels he has dictated the terms of the settlement. Diane can then shrug and say, "I guess that will be okay," and then quietly to herself murmur, "Checkmate."

THE GUILT WINDOW: USING GUILT TO YOUR ADVANTAGE IN DIVORCE

Another strategy for you to play in the game of psychological chess is a move I call the "guilt window." No matter who walks into my office, offender or victim, I explain the concept of the "guilt window." While this is not a legal term, nor is it something attorneys learn in law school, it is something everyone negotiating a divorce should be aware of. Ultimately, when the guilt window is present in a divorce, it can significantly cost the person who is allowing it to stay open. Depending on your role in the proceedings, the guilt window can either help you—or hurt you.

Guilty feelings can arise from any number of situations—cheating, stealing, lying, falling out of love, neglecting a spouse, focusing on a career, etc. Even the act of asking for a split can summon a cloud of guilt. In divorce, guilt is always present in one form or another. Whether you are the perpetrator or victim, there are some valuable ways to incorporate guilt into divorce-negotiation strategies—as well as prevent it from influencing you into making some long-term mistakes.

Maintaining an open window

Let us first consider the victim. Remember Blake from the intro? She is in a perfect situation to utilize the guilt window to her advantage. Odds are high that Blake's husband feels really guilty about cheating on his wife (rather, let me clarify, he feels terrible that he got caught). The guilt-ridden husband is now in the process of identifying any possible opportunity that will allow him to dig himself out of the hole he has created for himself. Blake, on the other hand, now has a brief window of time (a.k.a. guilt window) to take advantage of her husband while he knows (and cares) that he is in the doghouse and use the situation to her advantage. There is unlimited potential in divorce negotiations when infidelity and guilty feelings are involved.

However, as with most good things, there is a catch—it can be as if a flimsy toothpick is propping the guilt window open. You never know when the stick will snap and the window will slam shut. So there is a limited amount of time one may have when working to find a way in through the guilt window. Once the guilt window closes, the husband then becomes angry and begins to rationalize and project. This is typical of the accusation that arises: "If you gave it up more, then I would never have needed that other woman. This divorce is all your fault!"

The husband then goes further with this line of thinking. Not only did you *make* him cheat, but you also are responsible for making him furious with himself. Negotiating with an irate, cheating spouse who is rationalizing his bad decisions on the roller coaster operating inside his head is not easy. Right now, the husband is searching for every possible way to get back at you, because after all, you ruined his life—you bitch! Not to mention, it is much easier to be the victim than the perpetrator. When it gets to this point, the guilt window is closed and the chances of negotiating a great settlement are gone.

In a divorce, using guilt to your advantage is a fine art, and you absolutely must handle the situation delicately. It is necessary to tap into the guilt of the other party without allowing him to feel like you are taking him for a ride. He absolutely cannot believe he is being taken advantage of—because if he does get this vibe, then the affair becomes your fault. The secret is in identifying what will shut his guilt window. How far can you take things before you push him over the edge?

Be careful, because acting out of anger could be the very trigger that transforms a guilt-ridden, willing-to-negotiate husband into a vengeful, strategic fighter, and some psychological chess may be the only way to keep the window open long enough to get a good deal. Ultimately, this usually means the cheated-on spouse must hide their anger and appear to be the downtrodden, wronged party—no matter how hot you are running internally. I tell clients to think *Ghost* or *Terms of Endearment* or whatever movie makes you cry and ignore Fergie—"big girls do cry." You might seriously be envisioning using a hammer on a delicate piece of his anatomy (we'll deal with anger more in a bit)—but honestly, keep that to yourself. If you can keep your shit together, your wits about you, remain cool, and shed some tears on demand, it is more likely you will not lose the opportunity the guilt window presents.

Avoiding the guilt window

On the flip side, let's pretend you are the one having the affair and feeling remorseful. When I am representing a cheating spouse, my advice is equally as powerful—you need to avoid finding yourself in the guilt window. Yes, offering up some significant leverage to your soon-to-be ex-spouse might make you sleep better at night, but come on! Giving him 70 percent of the marital assets right now is not a long-term solution, even while it might appeal to your short-term sensibilities. Feelings of guilt are going to fade, but you know what will not? The realization that you gave your lazy ex-husband more than half your retirement for which you worked your ass off. That may haunt you forever.

Of course, up until this point, we have discussed a scenario involving cheating alone. It must be noted that infidelity is not always the cause of guilt in divorce. I regularly consult with clients who feel terrible that they fell out of love with their husband, as well as women who are dealing with serious internal strife because they had the audacity to focus on their career over their marriage. I have even run into clients who are ready to sign away their financial stability and future because they are the ones who brought up the subject of divorce.

Addressing guilt thoughtfully

Of course, every situation is different—and the details surrounding the guilt window should be considered on a case-by-case basis. Making a deal to alleviate one's guilty feelings is not always a bad thing. I pass no judgment on people who want to buy their way out of their guilt (after all, isn't that what rainy-day money is for?). So long as the client is making an educated, rational, and calm decision—and she is fully aware that the emotional state she is currently residing in is not permanent, no objections from me. If you can envision yourself five or ten years down the line making the statement, "I am really happy I gave him seventy percent of the assets in the divorce," then it is perfectly fine. If you do not feel confident in that statement, I would suggest you reevaluate the situation and spend a bit more time thinking about it before pulling the trigger.

Divorce might be laden with emotion, but it is a business decision. It is necessary to separate emotion from the workings of your rational mind— this is the only way to make smart decisions. Having this ability is the key to staying out of the guilt window. It is imperative that you examine the decisions you make today with eyes that can clearly see that your life will be different in the future. Down the road, you do not want to be beating yourself up for your decisions. So be honest with yourself. If you choose to buy yourself out of your guilty feelings, you can definitely do that, but recognize the rationale behind your choice and never look back at the price tag.

KICKING-DOG SYNDROME

Another emotional negotiation point I want to flag for you is what I call the kicking-dog syndrome (KDS). Big disclaimer here: I am a huge animal lover and love all dogs. That said, for some people, when they see a small dog walking down the street, there is an instinctual urge to kick it. Why? Because small dogs are seen as weak. And there are people who get angry at weakness. So I say this not to offend the lovers of Chihuahuas out there but to explain that if your spouse is a person who angers at weakness, be aware of that trigger while negotiating. If the power dynamic during the marriage was such that he ruled the roost and got angry when you played the helpless-female role, don't play that card during your negotiation, and instead find your inner German shepherd. But if your spouse is someone who wants to be the superhero and rescue the damsel in distress from the train tracks, then you do not need to worry about the KDS, and maybe you do play that role. To decide which character to play in the negotiation game is part of the psychological strategy.

THAT YOUNG SLUT IS ACTUALLY YOUR BFF

I often get calls from female clients who tell me, "I cannot believe that asshole is already dating some twenty-year-old bimbo!" My response is always, "That is fantastic!" Once they call me back after hanging up on me, I explain, "It is much easier to divorce someone who is in a happy relationship with someone else than a sad, lonely soon-to-be ex who is moping around thinking about how they will never make love to an-other woman and just obsessing about ways to win you back." An un-happy ex will just drag on the divorce process, play on your sympathies, and he might very well refuse to put that final signature on the dotted line. Alternatively, you can have an angry ex who will sit at home and think of ways to make your life miserable while sticking pins into voo-doo dolls with a picture of your face stitched on their heads.

Sexual pride can play a key role in this complex stage of the divorce process. An ex who knows you no longer want to have sex with him might feel increasingly miserable learning that you *do* want to have sex with someone else. But a happy ex, who realizes he can now openly date the types of pretty girls he could not get in high school, is great for your divorce, now that he has a nice car, he opens the door for them, can af-ford a fancy dinner with a full bottle of wine, and has left the awkward-ness of his teenage years behind him.

So if a hot, young thing is flirting with him, you should count your blessings. In the long run, and especially if you have children together, you will want this man to build a relationship with an emotionally healthy, sensible woman. However, for now, anyone who makes him smile enough to fend off fantasies of making your life miserable will be your best ally. A joke I often make to clients is: "The best money you can spend is to pay someone cute to date your ex while going through the divorce." Naturally, I am not advising you do that, but it does serve to bring the point home. Bottom line: dealing with happy people is less of a pain, and divorce is not the exception.

However, when it comes to your dating life, I have seen lawyers who advise clients not to date until the divorce is final, but I know you are human and the divorce experience is bad enough—why make it worse? What if you miss out on the next love of your life just because you were trying to have a clean divorce? I am fine when people date during a divorce if they want to. Going through the process of ending your marriage is difficult, but if you are putting your life on hold and depriving yourself of fun or other relationships, then it will just be that much harder. I find that your mind-set may be better in your negotiations if you also know that you are not going to end up an old maid living in your mom's basement with twelve cats.

That said, you should not be sharing your dating escapades with your ex. Therefore, online dating could be problematic, as posting identifiable info on dating sites is a tricky issue. While you are in the little purgatory that separates the kingdom of the married from the land of the divorced, make sure your dating life stays private. Met a dream of a man and cannot wait to tell your girlfriends? Great! But wait, one of them is the wife of your soon-to-be ex's best friend. . . . If there is the slightest chance that word about your dating activities might reach his ears, then keep your lips shut!

When interacting with your ex—act like men are the last thing on your list. Do not talk about going out and having fun. In his mind, he will see images of men trying to get in your pants, even if you say you went to the opera. . . . Strategy is the name of the game. The benefits of keeping your dating life quiet will be twofold: on the one hand, you will spare your estranged husband's feelings, and on the other, you will contribute to his positive attitude during negotiations. The last thing you want is a man who thinks you left him to start dating other, sexier, more interesting, younger, better men. The pious woman who has no time to think about anything other than her children is the image you want to project. Again, psychological chess.

WANT A NEW PAIR OF EARRINGS?
ANGER AND RETALIATION IN DIVORCE

What happens if your spouse is not swayed by your butter bomb, nor is he feeling guilty about cheating, he has kicked a bunch of small dogs, is so repulsive no one else will date him, and found out you are dating his old roommate from college? What if he is the irrational asshole who is willing to burn down the house just to make sure you do not get half of it? My advice when your spouse is "that guy" is to get out as quickly and painlessly as possible—even if it costs you a few bucks. I have represented those spouses who will fight to the death and those spouses who want to escape them. If you know that your spouse is totally incapable of acting rationally (under any circumstances, even if it costs him money) then you need to plan your escape route and get out.

A client—let's call her Amy—walked into my office with a very distinct request. Meeting my eyes directly, she said, "I want you to chop his balls off, and I want to wear them as earrings!" (Frankly, I can only imagine what she would have wanted as a matching necklace.) Amy was a client who was willing to fight to the death and take no prisoners. At the end, her perseverance worked to the degree that we got her a good settlement. However, after paying legal bills and therapy bills, I wonder if taking a bath in the cash she received felt as good as she thought it would. It is pretty common for someone to come to me seeking blood, and I am quick to point out we can definitely do that. In the world of divorce law, anger and the need for revenge—actions fueled by emotion in general—can run up some very big legal bills. So, my follow-up question to my clients when they request blood is, "Do you want to pay for your kid's college or mine?"

Ultimately emotions make us insane—and when we are running on emotional urges, we can act erratically. Think about it. Remember when your best friend was "blinded by love" and voluntarily moved in with a drug-addicted felon because "he is so hot! And the sex is amazing. He said he will never steal again and is done with drugs"? And we all know how that turned out.

The same holds true with anger and revenge. Facing a divorce, you feel so hurt; your heart is damaged. Your mind obsessively plays on repeat—searching to find ways to hurt that person as much as they hurt you. In turn, because you are blinded by anger, the value of money and peace of mind fades behind the bright, sparkling allure of giving that bastard just what he deserves.

THINK AHEAD: IS IT WORTH IT?

It is hard to rid yourself of anger—I get it; we have all been there. However, there are strategies for dealing with it. It is necessary to recognize anger and its place in your life while knowing it also affects one's ability to make rational, levelheaded decisions. When you attempt to negotiate your divorce while you are simultaneously fuming with anger, it is impossible to envision the reality of your future. It is necessary to visualize how your future self will feel about the decisions you make today. Looking forward allows you to temporarily set aside damaging emotions—at least long enough to make smart choices.

When you have the feeling of wanting to tear him apart, I want to step back and breathe for a second. Then I want you to think about your kids. How do you want your kids to describe your divorce from their dad twenty years from now? Do you want them to say, "My mother absolutely hated my father. They would fight all the time, and I was totally caught in the middle!"? Or would you rather they say, "No big deal. I liked going to Dad's new place every other weekend and I got double presents on my birthday!"? Yes, it can be incredibly difficult to step out of the anger and place your hurt to the side as you attempt to look through your child's eyes and consider his or her perspective. No one wants to fuck up their kid, and the realization that your actions today could impact her twenty years down the road can truly be eye-opening. Therefore, understand that making rational decisions, not emotional ones, is the key to preserving the future for both yourself and your children.

BIZARRE AND COSTLY BATTLES

What exactly happens when you make divorce-negotiation decisions that are fueled by emotion? Here is an example for you. A very wealthy client of mine—let's call him Bret—was absolutely furious with his spouse throughout their divorce proceedings. We were at the point where we had negotiated everything and finally were down to the last item—the wife's beloved grandfather clock. Bret did not want the ugly clock, but he was well aware of its emotional importance in his wife's life. And he was set on exploiting that.

Overall, the case was complex and involved more than twenty million dollars in assets, and it took us close to a year to get to a settlement. Bret was willing to throw that all away, along with tens of thousands of dollars in legal fees, to spar over a grandfather clock worth a grand total of eight hundred dollars. His goal? He wanted to set it on fire, make a video of it as it burned, and then send the clip to his ex-wife.

In the end, Bret did get the grandfather clock. While I never saw the video (I am sure he made it), I do not know whether winning felt as glorious as he expected it to. What I do know is that the cost-benefit analysis of his case was outrageous. Bret was completely aware of what he was spending to get this clock, and he simply did not care. People can be scary when they truly do not care about the consequences. He was blinded by rage.

COUPLES FIGHT OVER CRAZY THINGS

In my time as an attorney, I feel like I have seen it all. In some of the divorce negotiations I have overseen or heard about, there have been squabbles over the following seemingly petty items:

- An email address made of their combined names

- The cash value of a single breast implant

- A phone number

- Football season tickets (when the other spouse only likes to watch the commercials at the Super Bowl)

- Wanting three dinner plates from the wedding china because the husband knew taking three away meant that the wife would be one plate short when hosting her family

- Shoe collections

- A donated kidney (I kid you not.)

It is not my style to ask a client to shed his or her principles, but I do explain that having principles can be pretty expensive. After all, is fighting for six hours over a $1,000 painting—at a lawyer's rate of $750 per hour—worth it? In the end, it might be, at least to you. I encourage you to choose your battles wisely.

THE PSYCHOLOGICAL COST OF WAR

People want to quantify fault, but a judge (especially a divorce judge) is unlikely to be able to do that. Revenge does not only run up an attorney's bill and empty your pockets; there is more to it than that alone. Litigation has a real and tangible psychological effect on you, your physical and mental health, and the lives of everyone around you. Attacking your husband in a divorce is stressful enough on its own. When he makes the decision to fight back—giving it to you blow for proverbial blow—your angst, worry, irritation, and fury will escalate to new heights. Divorcing wives must ask themselves whether winning the Lamborghini is worth developing an ulcer and if it justifies the sleepless nights. Divorce litigation is not easy, and the psychological strain (along with the physical side effects) it can cause can be debilitating.

Like fighting in any war, there is PTSD when it is over. You would be naive to think that (even if you "win") you will walk away from this experience better for it.

Ultimately, and more often than not, revenge does not live up to the grand expectations you create in your mind—when you feel like you got your "just pound of flesh," it is usually anticlimactic. Consider what vengeance really means to you. If you want him to feel as hurt as you do, that may not happen—he simply might not care, or worse, he could enjoy seeing you go nuts. No amount of money or litigation is guaranteed to deliver the results you are fantasizing about. As time marches on—two weeks later, six months later, a year later—life changes. You might meet someone new, make an exciting career move, or have a new opportunity present itself that now fills up your days and occupies your thoughts. In turn, the anger dissipates—and eventually disappears. Would you rather enjoy your new life and the incredible deal you got in your divorce, or pay for the uncertain satisfaction of revenge?

WHEN REVENGE IS WORTH IT

Is revenge or simply the principle of "getting even" ever worth spending thousands in attorneys' fees and assets? Some clients believe if they do not fight to the death now, they will never forgive themselves and will forever feel that their husband took advantage of them. Yes, these feelings are real and important to consider. There are times when going to war is the right thing to do. But as with anything in divorce, there is no hard-and-fast rule for how this is determined. Every case is different.

If getting revenge is more valuable to you than money, plenty of attorneys are going to be happy to fight for you (see the soldier attorney, page 102)—after all, they want to make money. Sometimes sticking up for yourself and threatening to take your husband for all he is worth will be enough to cause him to give in. So it may be worth a shot—but in this I recommend you assess your own appetite for stomaching risk. Are you a gambler?

Remember, the dream of vengeance is usually sweeter than the reality. Litigation is slow, expensive, and incredibly frustrating. Before making a rash decision, step back and do not only visualize your future but also try to envision your children's future. Make educated, rational choices. In the end, you may decide taking him to the bank is not such a good idea. On the other hand, maybe a new pair of earrings is exactly what you need.

IT IS EASIER TO DIVORCE A CALM PERSON THAN A CRAZY PERSON

I am not a psychiatrist, and this book is not meant to claim to make any diagnosis of you or your spouse. But certain people are far more high-drama than others, are more volatile, more prone to whiplash-causing escalation, less prone to being rational and thus more difficult to reason with. Odds are they like being bombed with butter—in their minds, they walk around slathered in it—but the whole appealing-to-rationality side takes a lot more work.

But acting rationally assumes rational goals, and it's worth considering that their goals may actually be different here. Consider the spouse who does want time with the child, just not all the time—this person is very happy to lead their life and is very happy to have the child fit into it when it's convenient. He would never actually word it that way, but if he could be honest with himself he would. The actions are clear—you are the primary caretaker, you can do most of the work, and he can post cute pictures on social media for everyone to coo over (don't read the comments, they will just annoy you). But because he has such little time with his child, there has to be a reason why—and the reason can't be, "I can take or leave my kid"—that would not sit well at parties. So you become the reason—*you're* difficult, *you* want to take all his money, *you* won't let him see his kid. You're the villain—which puts him in the sweet spot that he lives for—the victim.

I am sorry to say that he will be the victim for the rest of your life. Nothing will ever be his fault, and everything will always be yours. Which means that this ex will be operating with perverse intentions— not to maximize time with his kid but to maximize showing the world how mean you are and how sad and downtrodden he is.

It is for these people that the rules of psychological chess are even more important. It will be hard to stomach, but if you can do everything to praise and flatter him and dial back on pointing out that he has passed on taking five of the last twelve parenting weekends, you will save yourself a lot of stress and time.

Yes, these people are time sucks. In many cases they are likely clinical narcissists, but since, again, I am not a psychiatrist, I can classify them only as high-drama individuals. They will be the ones posting hard-to-miss blind items on their Facebook walls (like a mess of photos from an elaborate Father's Day brunch with a framed photo at a seat for the missing child, or innocent inquiries about if anyone knows a specialist in parental alienation). You will find yourself with a collection of screenshots from their invective-filled text messages, vainglorious social media, repeated ignored calls, and time-stamped photos proving he was exactly where he said he was when you claimed otherwise.

It will be exhausting—and the harder you try to be nice and agreeable, the more this person may drag you down the slippery slope of his drama, because engagement is exactly what he wants. The best course of action is to drastically minimize your communication and enact firm boundaries, right from the start. Put his email address behind a filter that you check twice a week, refuse to communicate by text beyond child-related scheduling communications for something happening on that day, and do not pick up the phone when he calls (because, above all, you need a written record and he will leave a message or send a text if it is really important and because strict adherence to the truth is likely not their thing). Stay neutral but nonengaging except insofar as you need to make plans for your child (insofar as you can).

This is generally what is known as "gray rocking"[1]—that is to say, making yourself as invisible and interesting to them as a gray rock. It's not ignoring him, because you do have a child with him (although ignoring him would be bliss—alas, that would also be catnip: remember Glenn Close's iconic line in *Fatal Attraction*: "I will not be ignored!"). Rather, it's about absolutely minimizing any opportunities or opening for drama and escalation.

Bomb with butter, sure, but the best way to proceed with an antagonist like this is by referring everything to your attorney and getting it done as fast as possible. Unfortunately, as Nora Ephron noted, you will always be divorced from this person—but at least you won't be married to him anymore.

While my parents were both psychotherapists, I am not pretending that I absorbed their education and license in the womb. But what I can tell you is that over the last twenty years I have been divorcing people, I have seen a lot of things that work in divorce and a lot of things that do not. And it would be naive to walk into this divorce process thinking that the law alone will protect you and/or that you will see "justice." It is just not that simple. While I have said that you are best served not letting your emotions dictate your decisions, you can hope that your soon-to-be ex has not read this book and may not have heard or be capable of hearing this type of advice. So play the game of psychological chess and play it wisely—it is the best move you can make.

You Do Not Need to See the Inside of a Courtroom to Get Divorced

A good compromise is one where everybody makes a contribution.
—ANGELA MERKEL

You have decided you are getting divorced, are determined to participate in self-care during the process and have your chess board set up. This would be the time when you would think you would pick up the phone and call an attorney. But there is a step you should take before you do that. (I know it is not great for business for me to tell you to hold off calling an attorney.) Before you start your Google search for "best divorce attorney in the land," you need to know specifically what you are looking for so you do not end up with an attorney who spends a ton of money on search engine optimization but is not a good fit for your case. You need to understand your divorce-process options so you can decide how you are going to get divorced and then choose the attorney best suited for you.

MULTIPLE-CHOICE TEST: WHICH DIVORCE PROCESS IS RIGHT FOR YOU? (A) LITIGATION (B) MEDIATION (C) COLLABORATIVE LAW (D) ALL OF THE ABOVE

As in most things in life—rarely is "one size fits all" the best option. This is especially true when it comes to ending a marriage. One of the first things I tell my clients is that it is not necessary to see the inside of a courtroom in order to secure a divorce. Yes, you may end up in court, but you don't have to start there. Pace yourself, plan ahead, and strategize. Making educated choices will save you a lot of time, money, stress, and legal fees (not to mention therapy bills as well).

Traditionally, there are three ways to divorce—mediation, collaborative law, and litigation. *Mediation* involves the use of a neutral mediator who will help you and your spouse navigate divorce decisions together, often with an attorney assisting in the background. *Collaborative law* utilizes a team of attorneys, a neutral financial expert, divorce coach(es), and a child specialist (if applicable) to ensure you reach an agreement that works for everyone. If these two voluntary processes are not a good match for you, then *litigation* is the next option (which includes under its umbrella good old-fashioned lawyer-to-lawyer negotiations). However, even with litigation, there are no rules that say you have to end up in court—but it always remains an open option. If you try mediation and it does not work, you can move on to collaborative law. If collaborative law does not work—well, the courts do not close their doors to anyone.

The neutral navigator: mediation

Of the three divorce process options, mediation is typically the least expensive, as well as the route that has fewer opportunities to be acrimonious (not to say that everyone always plays nicely in the sandbox). Both spouses voluntarily choose the process with the goal of working together to reach an agreement. A neutral mediator helps the couple navigate the issues and make decisions, and each party usually has an attorney outside the process to advise them along the way. It is important to note that mediation is a self-selecting process and may not be right for everyone. To determine if mediation is right for you, you want to consider some things:

- <u>Financial transparency:</u> Are you in the financial dark? If your husband handles the finances and you believe he could hide money and not be truthful, mediation may not be the best process choice for you. There are ways to overcome this obstacle in mediation, but it is a concern you should discuss with your attorney when determining if mediation is the best divorce-process option for your situation.

- <u>Power imbalance:</u> Is there a huge power imbalance in your relationship? Sessions typically take place with only you, your spouse, and the mediator—attorneys are rarely present. Keeping that in mind, are you able to stick up for yourself if your attorney is not present? Will your husband be able to bully you into a settlement? Be honest with yourself when answering these questions. You need to make sure you can be present and vocal in the process to ensure it works and you achieve a favorable outcome. I must stress that being able to have a voice in mediation is crucial for the process to work. Consider this analogy: view the final divorce agreement as if it is a tower. It is constructed from bricks that are composed of smaller, individual agreements around individual issues. Each issue builds upon the previous one. Without a lawyer there, you may feel pressure to just agree to things to keep it going, and since you really do want to get this done, you "yes" all his asks, and so the mediation moves on to the next proverbial brick. Your spouse makes decisions around your agreements. It is only after the session is over, when you have met with your attorney (who tells you that you cannot just agree with everything to avoid confrontation) that you realize your error, and you backtrack. You remove a brick, and the entire tower collapses. The mediation fails, and we are back at square one (except your spouse is now angry that so much time and money was wasted). Your active presence and communication during mediation is essential for the process to work. And it has to be done right the first time.

- <u>Owning decisions:</u> Many couples expect (and want) mediators to be the judge and jury and make decisions for them. That is not the mediator's role nor how mediation works. You are the decision maker, regardless of whether you like to make hard decisions or if you would rather avoid them. Some clients feel that they would rather fight for what they want in court and give the judge the final say. That way, if the judge renders the final verdict there is no guilt surrounding whether they made the right decision. But if you can make and own your decisions and take responsibility for them, mediation could be a good option.

- <u>Game face:</u> Will you be able to contain your emotions and stay focused in the room? Mediation may seem like a long-awaited opportunity for you to get things off your chest, but these meetings are not glorified, expensive therapy sessions or wrestling mats for spouse bashing. Arguments will happen, yes, but mediation is all about moving forward—so you have to be ready to do it and not be filled with pent-up resentment when you do. (Can you resist bringing up his slutty young girlfriend at every turn? Again, be honest.) Mediation is a platform to facilitate the divorce agreement, nothing more. Keep your game face on and your eye on the prize.

- <u>Use your attorney:</u> Are you willing to use your attorney during the mediation process? You should! I understand you may have chosen mediation to keep costs down, and speaking to an attorney costs money. However, the goal of mediation is to draft an agreement for the attorneys to review and approve. Therefore, your attorney needs to be on top of this process in order to adequately represent you and your interests. Even if you feel good about how things are going, you still need that arm's-length third-party sign-off and someone who looks at the case from your vantage point. Remember the wife who said yes to everything to avoid confrontation and then changed her mind after speaking to her attorney? It blew up her mediation tower [insert the sound of a building crumbling]. Regular communication with your attorney can save the mediation.

Mediation is a very attractive option for many high-net-worth and celebrity couples because it is all confidential and you do not have to worry about your children reading the details of your divorce on Page Six of the *New York Post*. It is well known that Jennifer Garner and Ben Affleck turned to mediation to resolve the details of their divorce, which I am sure was in part to keep it all confidential and respectful. If you are not sure whether you can handle mediation, I recommend you try one session. The worst that can happen is that you wasted one hour of time and have to pay the mediator's fee. The best that can happen is that you realize this is a divorce process where you reach an agreement with your spouse in a manner that saves money, time, and possibly your sanity.

A team of experts: collaborative law

The wave of the future may well be collaborative law, a brilliant alternative to mediation that provides guidance using a team of trained specialists. Attorneys and other specialists go through a lot of training to be able to practice in this method.

Like mediation, the collaborative process is voluntary. Both parties must agree to enter the process. However, unlike mediation, both attorneys attend the sessions along with other members of the team, often including a neutral financial adviser, a divorce coach or coaches, and a child specialist. The expert advice and guidance of the team members helps to drive the entire process forward. I tell clients, "I am the most expensive player on the team—why wouldn't you use experts who have lower billable rates and do only this day in and day out?" It seems like a no-brainer to me.

The catch in the collaborative model is, if the process breaks down (and either party can decide they do not want to do it anymore) and they decide they want to litigate, then neither party can be represented by their collaborative attorneys in court. Everyone needs to start all over again with new counsel. Hence, the rub.

In the collaborative process, neutral financial advisers are exceptionally valuable players. Not only do they cost less than paying an attorney to handle the finances, but they also can boost the confidence levels of both sides. If your spouse handles the money and you are not financially savvy, having a neutral financial expert explain the numbers provides comfort, as you will know the numbers are not being manipulated. On the other hand, if you are the financial genius, you will want someone to explain the details to your spouse so he knows you are not taking advantage of him.

The psychological components of divorce can be harder than the legal and financial issues combined. This is where the divorce coach comes in. Some people who already have a therapist will often resist the idea of a divorce coach. "I do not have the emotional capacity for more than one therapist in my life," they say. But divorce coaches are not there to act as typical therapists. I often call divorce coaches in the collaborative process the "translators" because while you both may have started out speaking in English to each other when you married, by the time you get to my office you are now speaking Mandarin while your spouse is speaking Portuguese. So the divorce coach helps make sure the husband and wife are speaking the same language again and actually hearing and understanding each other. They often handle child custody issues and emotional matters. Divorce coaches are great at keeping things as calm as possible and often charge less than what an attorney would bill to handle these same aspects of the case.

Many collaborative-law divorces also incorporate a child specialist who works to establish parenting schedules and manage parent-child issues. The child specialist can meet with the children. They generally work with the parents and divorce coach to resolve access scheduling, custody, and other child-related issues and bring the child's voice into the room, without Sam having to miss soccer practice to attend meetings.

As opposed to mediation, the collaborative process protects you from making bad deals to some degree. Power imbalances have less of an effect on the outcome. Those who do not feel comfortable speaking out can sit quietly in the corner and whisper to their attorneys, "I do not agree with that," and let their attorney be their voice.

Collaborative law is also a popular option among celebrities and other public figures. I am informed that Robin Williams used collaborative divorce to end his nineteen-year marriage to Marcia Garces Williams. Billionaire Texas financier T. Boone Pickens also engaged in the collaborative process to end his fourth marriage (I guess he learned his lesson on divorces one through three).[1] Like in mediation, high-profile couples want to keep the details of their divorces quiet, and collaborative law can accomplish that goal.

Collaborative law is a great option when mediation is not going to work and you do not want to go to court. I have seen the collaborative law process save some very difficult cases from what I know would have been drawn-out litigations. I once had this woman—let's call her Andrea—come to me and was practically foaming at the mouth about her desire to screw her husband (retaliation for him screwing someone else). Therefore, you can imagine how surprised I was when she ended the consultation saying, "So I would like to try collaborative law." Now,

I am rarely one to suggest litigation, but I expressed to her my shock that she said she wanted to sit in a room with a man she just described as despicable and after mentioning Lorena Bobbitt as her hero. Andrea emphasized that she did not want to go to court and wanted to give it a try. So we did. The first session was rough, and I kept all scissors and knives safely hidden. However, after she had a few sessions with the divorce coach, the transformation in my client was amazing. I am not going to say that she still would not have enjoyed wearing his balls as earrings, but she was definitely calmer and able to realize that her anger was not self-serving and she needed to get over it for the sake of her kids (and for her own sake). The case ended with a very fair settlement for Andrea (she slipped through the guilt window before it snapped shut), and while she and her husband did not walk off hand in hand, I do truly believe that they will now be able to, together, walk their daughter down the aisle one day. Thank you, collaborative law.

GOING TO BATTLE: LITIGATION

Many clients have engaged in the litigation fantasy laid out here at one point during their divorce. They imagine that once they take their soon-to-be ex to court and the judge hears what a bastard he is, they will be awarded everything they are asking for and the beloved Porsche will also be thrown in for good measure. Clients honestly believe that justice will be immediately served—case closed—straight to commercial. Just. Like. That. Ultimately, it is then my responsibility to explain to a client that having their "day in court" does not unfold like an episode of *Law & Order*. Rarely does this outlet offer the emotional satisfaction they are craving, so the reality of the courtroom is something that clients must be prepared for.

While there are many injustices that can occur during divorce proceedings, the one that clients believe a court will address are extramarital affairs. "When the judge hears that he slept with my sister (who he always knew I hated) in the same bed where our children were conceived, that judge will hand me my husband's balls on a silver platter," a scorned wife will say.

No. That will not happen.

In fact, at least in New York, it would most likely not even be a relevant factor that can be brought to the judge's attention. New York, along with other states in the United States, are no-fault states, which means you do not need to prove the grounds of fault in order to get divorced. Many states do still have grounds for divorce on their books, but if I try to bring a divorce on the grounds of adultery (for example)—the judge would be chopping off my figurative balls. Bottom line, judges do not have the time, patience, or legal obligation to listen to your drama. Even when fault grounds did play a role in divorce, judges have heard it all before and are so jaded that they will not be surprised by your tale. The legal standard is that a case needs to "shock the conscience of the court" to effect asset distribution, and I can tell you from firsthand experience that a judge's bar to have his/her conscience shocked is pretty high. Sagas such as the Anthony Weiner and Huma Abedin disaster or the Tiger Woods divorce would not faze these judges. To give context, cases where asset distribution was affected involve husbands who hired hit men to kill their wives and men who beat their wives with barbells in front of their children. So, unless your case involves elements like these (and if so, please put this book down and call the police), the odds of your case shocking a judge is slim.

The legal irrelevance of an affair is a hard pill for clients to swallow. It is devastating to learn the secret diary that has been kept detailing all the times a husband came home late smelling of perfume or displaying his sexting messages (and any other type of logging of evidence) does not play a significant role in the legal process. This does not mean all your snooping and detective work was a waste. Certainly, it can provide significant leverage in negotiations. However, be strategic and do not bring his infidelities to the judge's attention believing it will be a game changer, because once your ex-husband sees the judge and the court could not care less, he will not worry about your evidence either.

Litigation is not a speedy process, and it is very expensive

Litigation can be long and drawn out and very pricey. While negotiation (be it kitchen-table talks, collaborative law, or mediation) feels time-consuming, it is more often than not still quicker and cheaper than actual courtroom litigation.

Court appearances can take many hours, and while you may see the judge for only a few minutes, you will be paying your attorney while you wait around playing on your phone and she schmoozes with other attorneys in the hallway talking about the latest sale at Saks. So, assuming you get started at 9:00 a.m. and get out at 1:00 p.m., you have spent $3,000 (assuming $750 per hour billable rate). Of course, if your case gets held over through lunch, then you have to come back after lunch. You might not be done until the end of the day, which means that you just spent a full eight hours with your attorney at her billable hourly rate!

Now, if you are the monied spouse, there is a good likelihood you may be paying most of the legal bills (or they will be paid from marital funds). I also want to note that if you are working with a partner at a firm who brings an associate with her, then you are paying that associate attorney's rate as well. All in all, it is possible you could be paying for four attorneys at a combined rate of over $2,000 per hour, which means that simply meeting the judge and being told to settle has cost you $8,000. And you could not even mention your ex's affair!

Sometimes litigating can be a strategic move. If it is your ex who will be paying the majority of the legal bills, then that is $8,000 out of his pocket. You may not have been able to witness the tongue-lashing you were hoping for, but you still got to hurt him below the belt—in his wallet (what were you thinking?)

DISCOVERY, DEPOSITIONS, AND ALL THE REST

After you have handled some of the initial steps in your case, what comes next is the phase called "discovery." In general, discovery is a pain in the ass—but it is necessary. The joke is that on discovery, you rarely really discover anything meaningful. Discovery is the time where you are required to gather all your financial information and present it to your attorney, who will bate-stamp it (meaning they number each page of the discovery), index it, and present it in a nice neat package to the other side.

The first step of figuring out what assets and liabilities exist is having both parties complete a statement of net worth where you (and your spouse) will list all assets, liabilities, income, and expenses. This is a key document in any divorce and the basis upon which a divorce settlement is often crafted. Following the statement of net worth exchange, the attorneys will send each other document demands, which are requests for financial documents that are usually associated with the assets and liabilities listed on the statement of net worth.

When I say this requires you to pull all your financial information, I mean it. You need to present everything. You will be required to gather information going back anywhere from three years to the date your marriage began, including bank statements, credit card statements, canceled checks (if you have them), travel receipts, your résumé, documents associated with any business(es) you own, documents evidencing your expenses, your passport, your vacation receipts, your Uber receipts (to explain why you spend $3,000 per month on Uber transportation when you have a BMW sitting in a $400-per-month garage), your clothing receipts, your organic grocery receipts, etc. This document-gathering stage usually takes anywhere from one month to eight months by the time all documents are gathered (especially if you have to subpoena documents from banks or gather old documents).

After you gather all the documents, now you get to engage in the fun activity of depositions! (I hope you can sense my sarcasm.) Depositions are when you, your ex, your attorneys, and a court reporter sit in a room together and you get to answer questions under oath. The questions will likely be about the financial documents that were produced.* Depositions will also usually cover the history of your marriage, how you met, and your educational background. There will sometimes also be thinly veiled questions regarding your financial—as well as nonfinancial—contributions to the marriage (such as child-rearing and homemaking). Questions about affairs or extramarital activities sometimes get snuck in if money was spent on them. This is where spouses think they will embarrass the other spouse enough into settling. However, as you recall from earlier in this chapter—affairs do not really matter (at least not legally). So when I have a client who is accused of spending too much money on lingerie for his girlfriend, I tell him to answer the question by being honest in what was spent and adding to the sentence "And she looked *amazing* in it." Be careful about asking questions you do not want the answers to.

For the monied spouse, financial disclosure in a divorce can be a logistical nightmare. As stated, you will be required to produce thousands of pages of documents on your business dealings and the like, which may be legitimate discovery demands or a fishing expedition just to torture you so you will cave in and end the fight (which is often the legal strategy). Also, when dealing with businesses, the fear of disclosure is very real because you may or may not have expensed your Birkin bag on the business account and you do not want to give your soon-to-be ex

---

*In New York, we are permitted to only conduct financial depositions. If you are litigating in another state, you may be permitted to ask non-financial depositions as well.

ammunition against you or your company. A proactive approach about confidentiality agreements when exchanging business materials may be necessary but can also be key.

For non-monied spouses, there is often a higher degree of uncertainty as to the marriage's financial picture, as these individuals are often not involved in managing the finances. There may also be a lack of transparency by the monied spouse about the annual household budget and the extent of marital assets. I call this being kept in the "financial dark." Of course, it is standard issue for many clients to panic when they are the party who is not in the financial know. There are always thoughts about hidden bank accounts or stacks of cash sitting around in a villa in the Cayman Islands. While I cannot say this does not happen, I can offer reassurance that it is much harder to hide assets than most people think. If your spouse works for a public company, you can often find out what his income is; if he is a W-2 employee, then it is even easier. Then through the financial-disclosure process, your attorney will review the financial documents he produces (at your attorney's request) and question your spouse about the monies at his deposition. So assume your spouse earns $800,000 per year as a W-2 employee and brings home around $400,000 per year after taxes and withholdings ($33,333 per month). However, you start to notice that instead of $33,333 being deposited into your joint bank account each month, you see only $23,333 going in there. So, at his deposition, your attorney will ask, "Where is the extra ten thousand dollars per month going?" This is when he better have a good answer (Bitcoin, anyone?) and if not, you may want to check for flight purchases to the Caymans. Hiding assets becomes more of an issue when you have a spouse who works in a cash business (restaurants and dry cleaners are the worst), but even then, a good forensic accountant can often find the goods.

TESTIMONY TIPS

While I am not looking to render legal advice, I do feel the need to provide some tips when discussing depositions and how I prepare my clients for testimony. When you are asked a question in a deposition or a trial, listen to the question and answer only the question that was asked. Seems simple, but it is not always so simple. Many clients believe they know what the question is that the attorney is going to ask as soon as she begins to ask it, so they answer the question they think the attorney is asking and stop truly listening to the question that is actually being asked. Remember the kid in school who raised his hand when the teacher was talking? That kid never answered the right questions because he was never listening to what the teacher was saying but instead was thinking about what he wanted to say. Also, if you are nervous the attorney is going to ask you about something, you may hear that question being asked when, in fact, it is not. So if the attorney starts the question of "When you were in the grocery store on September eighteenth—" and you blurt out, "Yes, that is when I met Pablo when he was squeezing the melons to see which were firm and one thing led to another . . . ," but the rest of the question was really "and you spent $823—was that all for food for your son's birthday party?" you provided ancillary or unnecessary information.

Another tactic I am a proponent of is silence. Many times, when I am the attorney taking the deposition of my client's spouse I will ask a question, wait for the answer, and then, prior to immediately asking a follow-up query, allow silence to permeate the room. The reason I do this is simple. Silence makes people uncomfortable, and when an individual is feeling antsy and silence abounds, they are more likely to keep talking. So a client will answer the very basic question of "Do you work?" with the answer of "Yes," and when I do not immediately ask a follow-up question but rather stare at the deponent as if I am waiting for more, sometimes I will get "And . . .and . . . I know I could be working more, but I was told not to work more so I would not earn much money when going through this divorce!" This gives me information that I did not request but received just the same. There is an old saying that goes "If you give someone enough rope, they will hang themselves with it." Do not commit deposition suicide.

Another deposition tip is that your deposition is not the place to prove your case. What often occurs is that a client wants to tell the other side all the reasons that he/she is right and explain further to the attorney why their client is an asshole. I once had this client—let's call him Michael—whose family owned pizza restaurants that went back generations. He and his brother ran the restaurants, and it was Michael's idea to expand the menu to include specialty pizzas and other Italian fare and to franchise. Michael met his wife (who was a hostess at one of the restaurants), and they got married fast and had kids even faster. For the last five years of their marriage (as Michael described it to me), his wife sat on the couch all day eating bonbons (he literally said that), directing the nannies around, while he was killing himself working like a dog to pay for said bonbons. Now, in the divorce, the wife had the nerve to ask for a lump-sum payment for his interest in his family business and for lifetime spousal support. At his deposition, he was insistent on explaining to his wife's attorney how hard he worked and how the wealth was all due to his having the right last name and working hard. He wanted to convince her attorney that her client was an entitled bitch and believed if he could sway her attorney, her attorney would talk some sense into his soon-to-be ex to take the deal that was on the table. Despite my consistently telling my client that his wife's attorney was not going to all of a sudden represent his interests (no matter how charming he may be), Michael believed what he believed.

Come deposition day, Michael took every opportunity to speak about how it was his brainchild to expand the restaurants and did not miss a chance to bash his wife. The question would be, "How many nannies do you employ?" He would say in a nasty tone, "My wife is so lazy, I am sure she hired ten nannies for two kids, and it is hard to keep track because she paid them in cash off the books. (Who wants to pay benefits?) I do not have time to pay attention to any of that stuff because I am working all the time. I just know she spends money like water. I have no idea what she spends—but I know it is a lot, and I don't like it!" The question would be "How much did you pay for your Porsche?" and he would respond with: "Well, I used the money that I earned from working twenty-three-hour days, which included every weekend. Do you know how much work it was for me to expand our menu and franchise? It did not magically happen, and there was no one to help me, so I had to do it all myself. I spent numerous sleepless nights coming up with those pizzas that made me millions, while your client slept like a baby. I earned every dime that I spent on that car!"

When we took a break for lunch, he was so proud of himself for "showing her" and looked to me for praise. But I was quite annoyed. I explained to him that we better settle the case now. He could not understand why I would say such a thing, since he "got everything good on the record." And I explained to him (for what felt like the fortieth time) that all of his self-serving comments will not see the light of day because we cannot use them to support our case, as they are his own testimony. However, what he did get on record was:

- His involvement with the children was minimal, since he said that he worked twenty-three-hour days and on weekends. Now it is more difficult to claim he was this involved dad when he makes his custody request.

- The appreciation (which was in the tens of millions) of what would have been his separate-property family business was in fact now active appreciation and due to his active efforts because he admitted to doing all the legwork for the franchising and menu expansion—efforts he expended during the marriage.

- He had no idea as to the amounts of money she claims she spends because he admitted that he does not pay attention and therefore it will be that much more challenging to then argue against her claimed budget.

- He admitted on a sworn statement that he pays the nannies cash off the books (although he will say she is the one who does it, but he knows about it, so he is just as guilty), which, while often done, is a big no-no.

- He thoroughly pissed off his wife to the point for no real gain and now she will be less likely to settle, as she is angry.

At a deposition, you can either tie (by not saying anything that damages your case) or lose (by saying something that damages your case), but you cannot win—Michael lost.

ADDITIONAL EXPECTATIONS

Throughout discovery it is likely you will also spend time in court conferences, checking in with the judge. There may also be motion practice, which means your attorneys will complete written and oral motions asking for various relief from the court throughout the litigation process. Motions can be very expensive, but I do find that because you are asking for specific relief, motion practice can (at times) help advance the case. What you need to watch out for is attorneys who engage in unnecessary motion practice. More often than not, there should be efforts made to resolve issues prior to running to the judge.

Trial preparation is another matter. While the majority of the work falls to your attorneys, there is work for the client to do as well. I know that when our office is in trial prep, I get the order-in menus ready because long nights are ahead. Depending on the nature of the case, the client may or may not be joining the attorneys for dinner. Additionally, if others are involved in the case and will be testifying on the client's behalf, there may be third-party preparation as well.

One of the hardest parts of trial preparation is that you need to work to seemingly predict what your ex and their witnesses will testify on—and be prepared to cross-examine them. Then, your attorney also needs to consider what you will be cross-examined on and prepare you accordingly. If you are nervous about the trial (which of course you will be), do not be afraid to ask your attorney questions about the process so you can assuage your concerns.

The next step is trial day. I often joke with the litigators in my office that "trial decisions are an urban myth." Realize that most cases settle, and even though you may have gone through all the steps identified in this chapter, few go all the way to trial to the point that the judge actually renders a decision. You might have spent tens or hundreds of thousands of dollars on attorneys' fees, but it will most likely be on the courthouse steps where your case is settled. It is estimated that 95 percent of cases settle.[2] Sometimes you are forced to settle even when you are ready for trial! I had a case once, years ago, that was set for trial and the judge made it very clear that he was not granting any adjournments and that we better be ready to call our first witness on day one of trial. My partner and I spent months preparing—nights and weekends. This was a complex financial trial, so we had experts and the other side had experts. My client had to cancel an important business trip to attend that day, and we have several witnesses who were being flown in from all over the country to testify. The day of trial came, and we went into the courtroom all suited up and ready to go with our many boxes of exhibits. As the attorney who spent so much time preparing our arguments and examinations, I was excited to have this trial and have my *A Few Good Men* moment. When we walked into court with our witnesses and experts, the judge called all the attorneys to the bench. He looked down at us from his perch and said, "I have a headache and am not trying this case today. Go out in the hallway and settle it." I was flabbergasted. I remember turning to my partner and saying, "So what do we do now?" and he said, "We go out and settle the case." So all the attorneys and the clients went to the hallway and proceeded to spend three hours negotiating a settlement. All the while, the experts (who were billing by the hour) sat around and chitchatted, and the witnesses tried to book flights back to where they came in from. My client was initially devastated that he spent so much money in legal fees paying for our trial preparation and that he rearranged his entire life to be ready for this trial. In the end, he was fairly happy with the settlement, but when you added the legal fees he had to pay, it was not as good of a deal. While I cannot say that this happens often, the moral of the story is that even when you are ready for trial, all it takes is a cranky judge who did not get enough sleep the night before to call off your trial, and all your money, time, and effort are wasted.

While I do believe there are times when litigation is required, more often than not your case will settle out of court. It is simply a question of whether you settle in the beginning of your case prior to expounding time and money, or if settlement occurs when all else has been exhausted.

Despite everything stated, it is important to understand that selecting the litigation process does not necessarily mean running right to the courthouse. More often than not, couples negotiate their settlement without seeing the inside of a courtroom and sometimes do it themselves at the kitchen table. So negotiations fall under the umbrella of litigation because it is not mediation or collaborative law and the cloud of litigation always looms overhead. So why would someone choose to go to court? There are times litigation makes sense from a purely strategic standpoint. If there is one common thread among all divorcing clients it is this: Everyone hates to pay legal fees (and who can blame them?). Therefore, if I am dealing with a stay-at-home mom who has a Wall Street husband, as I have used in examples, the odds are the husband will be responsible for the majority of the wife's legal fees, as he earns the income. If that is the case, then the husband will do all he can to avoid paying an attorney hired by his wife whose sole purpose is to make his life hell. Who wants to pay their torturer? So there is embedded leverage for the wife to threaten court because the husband will have an extra incentive to settle the case and avoid the heavy costs of litigation. This may be a reason for the wife to litigate or at least keep the option on the table. But keep this thought in mind—litigation can be emotionally taxing, so make sure when doing your cost-benefit analysis of litigation to factor in the expense of your therapy bills!

I must take a moment in this litigation section to speak about how incredibly damaging litigation can be to a family. While I understand there are times it is necessary and sometimes you have no choice because your spouse initiated the proceedings, I must advise you to avoid litigating your case if you can. The whole point of litigation (especially custody litigation) is to point out all the flaws in the other person and prove that he/she is not a good parent, or partner, or person. As discussed, this is done via motion practice, which I equate to basically creative writing. You take a statement that was once made (even if it was years ago) and weave it into the story that you are telling the court about your marriage. For example, imagine during a huge fight with your husband seven years ago, when you were both drunk, that your husband called you a "selfish bitch." What happens now is, in the motion papers your attorney writes describing your marriage, it will state something to the effect of "During the marriage the husband would drink excessively and when drunk would call the wife horrific names such as 'selfish bitch.'" Of course, it is not worth mentioning that you called him a "pathetic, loser asshole" first, which spurred his nasty response. It also will not be stated that he apologized profusely afterward, as it was not his nature to speak to you that way, while it was totally your nature to fight dirty. Once your husband reads that you threw something like that into motion papers and portrayed him to be something he is not—it will be very difficult to later try to coax him into a nice settlement or even be able to sit across the table from him at your son's graduation dinner.

IN LIFE, AS IN DIVORCE, THERE SHOULD BE OPTIONS

When all is said and done—I am a strong advocate of at least trying to resolve your case via an alternative dispute resolution process before running to court. There are great benefits to resolving your case via mediation or collaborative law rather than via litigation. To begin with, both processes are typically less expensive and faster than battling it out in court. In the alternative dispute-resolution processes, you have more control on the timing and the ultimate outcome and can really tailor outcomes to suit the specifics of your case. As they say, "A negotiator uses a scalpel while a judge uses a butcher knife." The alternative dispute methods allow for emotional issues to be heard in a way that a courtroom does not have the tolerance or time for. The likelihood of post-divorce issues is less when people come to their own resolutions rather than having a decision shoved down their throats. While I will speak about this more in the high-net-worth section—it applies to all people—one of the biggest reasons I recommend that people stay out of court is that it is the best way to not have your dirty laundry aired on Page Six of the *New York Post*. Privacy is much higher in closed-door settlements than it is if a case is litigated (ever wonder why we never get the real details of a celebrity divorce?). Even if you only resolve a few issues in mediation or collaborative law, but have to take some other issues to litigation, you have probably saved many thousands of dollars in legal fees. I consider any resolution coming out of mediation or collaborative law a success.

I encourage you to learn this important rule: the way you start your divorce is often how you will end your divorce. If you are going to go in guns blazing, recognize you will be fighting. It is difficult to suddenly play the peacemaker when you begin in an aggressive mode. It can happen, but it is hard. If you initiate with mediation and a nicer approach, you are more likely to complete the divorce in a civil manner.

Whether mediation, collaborative law, or litigation, it is nice to have options.

When Choosing an Attorney Remember that Dolphins Are Smarter than Sharks

I have learned that not diamonds,
but divorce lawyers are a girl's best friend.
—ZSA ZSA GABOR

So you have now chosen your process. Regardless of which option you selected, the hard part is now figuring out who is going to be the person/ firm that is going to guide you through the most difficult maze of your entire life. Is it a question for Siri or for your thousands of Facebook friends? And to make you feel even more vulnerable, you are probably not exactly trusting yourself in the "people reading" category these days, so how do you find the perfect lawyer/firm for you? I am not going to lie to you—it is not an easy feat, and it is possible that you may not even get it right the first time.

Often people find attorneys through word of mouth. A personal recommendation from someone you trust goes a long way. Whether it is your sister's friend's husband's brother or some random yoga mom who heard the news, everyone will have a name for you to call. But maybe you don't know anyone who has gone through a divorce, or maybe you don't want anyone to know your marriage is in trouble.

In that case there is always the internet as a resource for finding an attorney. My favorite internet story was probably about fifteen years ago (when internet research was sketchy) and I had a man—let's call him Adam—who said he found me on the internet and reached out to me, asking that I draft a prenuptial agreement for him. Because I thought this would be a smaller case (after all, who calls from the internet?), I thought it was perfect for my associate to do the consultation and I sat in to supervise. When we met this man, he reminded me of Mr. Rogers, sweater vest and all. He explained he was marrying his hairdresser (he was bald) and wanted to protect his real estate. I figured we were talking a basic one-bedroom condo or something simple like that. When my associate asked what type of real estate and what was the approximate value, Adam's answer was "real estate buildings worth approximately $40,000,000." That answer made me stop doodling on my notepad and look up. At the next meeting we had, this man's son attended (obviously having a vested interest in this prenuptial agreement). I pulled the son aside at one point during the meeting and said, "How did you let your father pick an attorney off the internet?" His answer—"My dad thought you seemed nice." Go figure.

As I said, that was fifteen years ago. Times have since changed, and probably about 20 percent of the cases that come into our office are from the internet. It is incredibly common for people now to find their attorneys off the internet, whether it be from simple Google searches or from reading an article an attorney wrote or seeing a media clip. I believe the internet to be a great source for people searching for a divorce attorney, because even if you hear a name from your book-club friend, you can look up that person and verify information about this attorney before you spend the initial consultation fee. You just want to be careful about the law firms that paint a pretty picture on the internet but do not have the substance behind them to back it up.

When looking for an attorney it is important to choose a specialist in matrimonial law. General practitioners may dabble in divorce here and there, but there are many nuances to matrimonial law. Would you go to a podiatrist to do brain surgery? No, you go to a specialist. Same rule applies to divorce. When you work with a specialist, it is almost a given that he or she knows the laws pertaining to divorce but are also familiar with the psychological aspects of divorce. A client crying in the office does not faze a matrimonial law specialist; it is all part of the process. (I keep a box of tissues in my office at all times—the soft ones, because this process is rough enough.)

In matrimonial law, there are many more solo practitioners than there are firms. You will likely find a solo practitioner unless you make the active decision to work with a firm. Solo practitioners generally appear less expensive on the surface than firms do, though the end result may not always work out that way. Partners will often use less expensive associates to do some of the lower-level work, so the blended rates of a partner and associate at a firm versus a solo practitioner doing everything may be similar (or even cheaper) in the end. Firms have more heads than one to bounce ideas off of and also have other attorneys in the office who can cover for your attorney if for some reason he or she is unavailable. It may be worthwhile in the beginning to meet with both a solo practitioner and a firm to find the best fit for you.

You also want to choose someone practicing law locally. If you live in a suburb, you may think that "lawyering up" with a big-city attorney who is located two hours from the courthouse will show you mean business—but it could be a strategic mistake. Similarly, if you live in a city and think it will be cheaper to hire an attorney who lives upstate with lower billable rates, that may not be wise either. You will want your attorney to be accustomed to the courts, judges, and other counsel around them. Let's face it—people are nicer to those they know. Additionally, if you use an attorney who operates outside your area, you may end up paying for travel time (which, at $750 per hour, can add up—think about the traffic costs!). Be up front in asking your potential attorney about travel costs and find out if it will be worthwhile to hire from afar.

Once you have a few attorney names, next comes the vetting. First check out the website to see if the attorneys appear to be professional. Reviews and peer recognition are good criteria to use when choosing a divorce lawyer online—be sure to see if the attorneys are recognized and rated by formal legal organizations such as Lawyers. com, SuperLawyers, the American Academy of Matrimonial Lawyers (AAML), or Best Lawyers. When considering a lawyer in a firm, also check out their partners and associates as well. Initial consults are incredibly important here, as you want to meet (or at least speak to) the person who will be representing you and whom you will be spilling your deepest darkest secrets to.

You want to hire someone within your financial means. Many non-monied spouses say, "I can pay for your consultation, but I am not going to be able to afford you afterward" and yet the marital net worth is $30,000,000. I then assuage their concerns by explaining that if one spouse has deep pockets and the other does not, the non-monied spouse is still entitled to an attorney who is on par with the one hired by the monied spouse. Courts refer to it as "leveling the playing field." If he is the so-called monied spouse, he will likely pay the majority of your legal fees or they will be paid out of the marital assets, which means that you are in essence contributing. The bottom line here? Hire an attorney who makes you feel comfortable, as long as he or she is financially in line with your spouse's attorney and within your family's financial means.

SOLDIER VERSUS ADVISER

When selecting an attorney, you need to ask yourself—Do you want an attorney who is going to fight for you no matter what, or one who advises you along the way (even if the advice is something you do not want to hear)? Some attorneys soldier for their clients. If you walk in and say,

"I want my husband to never see my children again," the soldier attorney fights for exactly that—even if he knows he is going to lose. These attorneys believe that you are the client and it is their job to try their best to get the client what the client wants—even if pigs do not fly. I must warn you to remain vigilant about attorneys who make promises to you in a first meeting and assure you they will deliver what you want. No attorney can make that type of promise to you, and if he or she is making soothing, cooing sounds to quell your fears, be leery, as it just might be a hard sell to sign you as a client.

Other attorneys may get more involved and will not automatically do what the client wants, saying, "You may have a terrible spouse, but a terrible spouse does not necessarily equate to a terrible parent. I am not going to fight for zero parenting time for Dad because you will lose." (Not easy to hear, especially when you feel that if he was such a good father, he would not have destroyed his family by sleeping with his paralegal.) This attorney is not going to fight just to fight and sees his or her role as your attorney to advise you—rather than marching straight into battle without looking back.

Different attorney types fit different client types. If you feel you will never sleep at night unless you fought as hard as you could fight (even if you lose), then a soldier attorney may be the right attorney for you. If you want to look at the bigger picture and can swallow the fact that you did not fight every battle and consider a favorable result as winning the war (even if he feels he won too), then an adviser attorney may be better.

BRAINS VERSUS BRAWN

I always chuckle (sometimes to myself and sometimes out loud) when someone comes into my office and says, "I need a shark divorce lawyer—are you a shark?" It is a common conception (I think misconception) that you need an über-aggressive attorney to "put my husband in his place." There may be attorneys out there who are more aggressive than others, but you need to be mindful of whether blind aggression is always wise or is it better to have a strategic attorney who only uses aggression when appropriate and when it is most meaningful. Any attorney who calls me up and starts yelling or carrying on, I think to myself, *What have you got to hide, buddy?* In my opinion, the good attorneys, really good attorneys, do not need to put on the show and dance. Their legal and strategic arguments stand on their own, and they do not need to be presented with a raised voice. Personally, I rarely yell. In fact, I have yelled about three times in my whole legal career at the opposing counsel, and I regretted it each time I did. I showed them that they got to me. My favorite lawyer trick (and I play it on my husband and children too) is that the more you yell, the quieter I become. I let you throw your temper tantrum, and when you are done (and sometimes I actually ask an attorney if he/she is "done," which has resulted in a dial tone), we can have a rational and productive conversation. I see yelling and being overly aggressive as a sign of insecurity and weakness. I am much more challenged by an attorney who knows what he/she is doing and thinks before speaking as opposed to the attorneys who come in guns blazing and just yell to yell and do not actually say anything meaningful (they are just loud). Personally, I believe divorcing individuals are best served by a balanced approach—someone who knows when to be aggressive and when it makes sense to play nicely in the sandbox. In my twenty years of experience in which I had swam with many so-called sharks, I often find they wind up dead on the shore at the end.

DIVORCE LAW IS A BUSINESS

Whether soldier/adviser/shark/dolphin—there exists an inherent conflict of interests between divorce lawyers and divorcing clients. What I mean by that is, the more clients want to fight, the more legal fees are incurred, and the more money attorneys make. While many attorneys want clients to settle their case because it is better for the client, the fact is that settlements hurt their financial bottom line. So although matrimonial attorneys are not permitted to be paid on a contingency basis (because they want to avoid a situation where the attorney has a vested interest in the outcome), it is somewhat unavoidable because of the way that the attorney/client relationship in matrimonial cases is structured. The more the pot is stirred, the more soup there will be for the attorney. Let's face it—divorce law is a business; let's not pretend it is not.

There are firms out there that have a very simple business model:

Step 1: Tell angry client that we will get them whatever it is they ask for in the initial consultation (e.g., his balls on a silver platter). Take a large retainer to fight the good fight.

Step 2: File legal motion after legal motion asking the court to give said balls on platter and in the process deplete the retainer fee.

Step 3: Lose legal motion after legal motion because the court does not chop off a cheating husband's balls.

Step 4: Client is upset because she keeps losing. Attorney says to client, "I just did what you said to do—I cannot help it if the judge does not agree with mutilation."

Step 5: Client fires attorney. Attorney does not care because attorney already made money. On to the next client and retainer. . . .

For some clients—they are fine with this model because they wanted a soldier attorney and needed to feel they fought the good fight to sleep at night. But this model is not good for many clients, and luckily, not every divorce attorney out there subscribes to that business model. There are attorneys out there who really do want to settle their cases because the attorney wants to feel good about what they are doing to help your family. Now, don't get me wrong—I am not saying these attorneys are hangin' with Mother Theresa—they still bill for their time. Under these attorneys' way of thinking, clients are less likely to feel screwed by the process (because they are not always fighting losing battles) and the attorney is less likely to get fired. If the attorney is not fired, there is more of a likelihood that the attorney will be referred future cases by their current clients and will make more money that way. So the former is a short-term business model, and the latter is a longer-term business model. But under both methods, the attorney makes money, because divorce law is a business.

WHOSE SIDE ARE YOU ON ANYWAY?

Not only is your divorce lawyer set up to be at conflict with your best interests (assuming you think that is settlement), the attorney also has another issue. The matrimonial field (at least in the pockets of New York that I practice, but I am sure this is the same no matter where you go) is pretty incestual—meaning everyone knows everyone else. For example, since my firm deals in the high-net-worth space, we have worked with practically every other matrimonial attorney who deals with similarly situated clients in New York City. So since we all know each other, we often work together on many different cases at the same time. This leads to clients being concerned that we may not want to fight extra hard against a particular adversary because if we push hard on your case, that attorney may be more difficult on the other case that we have together. Not to mention that in divorce actions (or prenuptial agreements) both sides need to be represented, so there are a lot of referrals back and forth to attorneys who know each other. If one attorney is a major source of business for the other attorney, they may not want to piss that attorney off with some of the aggressive positions you want your attorney to take. Or maybe there is a concern that the attorney does not want to take to the judge your argument about only feeding your dog organic foods because you have another case before that judge when you are taking the opposite position. Clients fear that because of the relationship that attorneys have with each other and the relationships the attorneys have with the judges, the attorney will be more concerned with protecting their professional reputations than they are with fighting your case.

I recognize these concerns fly in the face of the advice I gave before, about selecting attorneys who practice locally because of the fact that everyone knows each other. While I am not going to pretend that there are not attorneys out there who play favorites and it is something you want to be aware of, I maintain that the odds of a case ending with a favorable result increase when the attorneys do have a relationship with each other. Also, I can tell you that I have gotten into some vicious fights with some of my best attorney friends, and while we may go to battle in the afternoon, we can still have a drink that evening and leave the bad feelings in the courtroom.

Clients often also worry that not only is their attorney in bed with the other attorney, but there are concerns that your attorney will be swayed by your spouse. Sometimes you fear hiring a male attorney because you do not want your attorney to share your husband's love of football and bond over that. On the other hand, if you hire a female attorney she may be charmed by your husband's good looks and quick wit. I have had to assure clients over and over again that I will not fall in love with their husbands. While they may have seen their spouse as irresistible at one point, odds are I will not. So if your spouse tells a funny joke and I laugh, you do not have to worry that I am sneaking off to the file room with him after his deposition.

Bottom line: attorneys are people too and will have their own biases, relationships, personal histories, and opinions that they will bring to your representation of you during your divorce. Some of these relationships will be a good thing (such as the fact that your attorney has Sunday barbecues with the judge), and some may not be as good a thing. But at the end of the day, you need to trust/hope that your attorney will sprinkle all the goodwill fairy dust he/she has to get you the best deal possible.

YOU DO NOT HAVE TO BE POLITICALLY CORRECT WHEN CHOOSING YOUR ATTORNEY

Who you choose for your attorney is a very personal choice and may not be as simple as picking the person with the best pedigree. While you want to hire the best person for the job, there could be other psychological aspects at play that you want to consider when making your selection. For example, I once had a client tell me that she was hiring me because she thought her husband would find me attractive. Her theory was that her husband would not want to disappoint someone he found attractive, which would result in his offering her a better deal so I would not think he was a cheap asshole. Similarly, I have had a man tell me he did not want to hire me because I looked like one of his ex-girlfriends and his wife hated his ex-girlfriend and he feared it would make her hate me and make the case more difficult to settle. So I have been told that I was hired because I was a woman and also told that I am not being hired because I am a woman. Some people want to have the older gray-haired man in the room—and that is not discriminatory against my being a woman. Divorce-attorney selection is not politically correct—this is your marriage, your family, and your life. And you need to be comfortable, and you need to be strategic in deciding whether you want your spouse to be comfortable or uncomfortable with your attorney. Please realize, I am not telling you to simply hire anyone based on their looks, age, or their sex. I am advising you to look at the big picture and consider all the actors in the play when deciding who is the best walk-on character to add to the scene.

YOUR ATTORNEY INTERVIEW: INITIAL CONSULTATION

Once you have selected some potential candidates, you should try your best to meet them in person (if possible) or at least have a phone consultation. Many attorneys charge for this initial consultation (although some do not), so be prepared for that. Since you will probably be paying for this meet and greet, you should make the meeting as efficient and productive as possible.

When potential clients ask me how they should prepare for the initial consultation, I advise them to bring a list of their assets, liabilities, and history (last five years) of the family income, if possible. This does not mean that I need for them to bring copies of all their bank statements and canceled checks for the past ten years, nor do I require boxes of receipts from when they went to the supermarket or every Starbucks receipt. Let's stick to the basics.

I also ask clients to bring a list of every question that has been keeping them up at night (silly or not). No matter the thought or fear, I would like to know about it, and it helps when an individual can ask everything he or she is worried about. I believe one of the purposes of the initial consultation is to give the attorney enough high-level information in order to get a sense of your case, as well as highlight the case's potential strengths and weaknesses, and most important, calm your nerves so that you can sleep at night.

In the first meeting, it is your overall goal to figure out if you and the attorney can work together, if there is chemistry per se, and ultimately, if the attorney even wants your business. As we know, divorce is a business—the odds are good the attorney will be vying to sign you as a client. However, realize that it is a two-way street, and you must feel comfortable with the person, his or her approach, and expertise.

In an effort to assist you as you prepare for your initial consultation, I have compiled a list of questions that are commonly asked. You can add these to whatever list you create:

- How long will this take?

- How much will it cost?

- How do you bill? Is it hourly (which is common), and if not, what is the flat fee? What other expenses could there be? How often will I receive bills?

- Where are the strengths of my case?

- Where are the weaknesses? (This is a time for honesty on the attorney's behalf.)

- How much experience do you have with cases like mine (high net worth / middle net worth / lower net worth; custody cases; custody cases with special-needs children; spouses who have cash businesses; cases with prenuptial agreements, etc.)?

- Will I be working with just you, or will other associates from your office work on my case? If so, do I get billed for everyone's time?

- How can I keep my costs down?

- What are your expectations of clients?

- Based on the background information I provided, is now a good time for me to get divorced?

- How should I tell my spouse that I want to get divorced?

- Is there anything I should not be doing while I am figuring out whether I want to divorce?

- Have you worked on cases with my spouse's attorney before? Do you know the judge in our case?

- Does your practice focus only on family law?

- Can I negotiate directly with my spouse during the divorce process?

- If I cannot reach you, is there someone else in your office I will be able to speak with in the event something comes up? How responsive will you be to emails and calls on off hours—can I expect same-day responses?

- What is the amount of the retainer? What is your process for handling a surplus of funds on the retainer?

- Is there anything I should be doing right now to prepare for this divorce?

- What would the next steps be if I wanted to move forward?

- Are you an advocate or a warrior?

Most clients who find themselves sitting in an attorney's office for the first time are understandably scared and confused—and probably do not want to be there. These individuals could be looking to the attorney to sprinkle some fairy dust and simply make their ex disappear (or if not disappear, then at least put an anti-asshole spell on him to turn him into a rational and decent human being). Yes, when clients have an air of desperation and a tear-streaked face, it can be tempting for the attorney to tell them everything will be okay and that they will get everything they are looking for in this divorce (remember the first business model we spoke about). The initial consultation can be a great time to see if this attorney will be able to give you the tough love you may require during the life of the divorce, while still making you feel supported and protected.

THE TWO BIG QUESTIONS:
HOW MUCH AND HOW LONG?

Two of the most popular questions I hear from clients at initial consultations are: "How long is this going to take?" and "How much is it going to cost?" My tongue-in-cheek response is, "Tell me how long it will take for you and your spouse to agree, and then I can tell you how long it will take." If any attorney tells you in your initial consultation that the divorce process will take "six months, two days, and thirty-eight minutes" run, do not walk, from the office. No attorney can predict with any accuracy just how long a divorce will take. What he or she may be able to offer you is an average amount of time as to how long a case can take once the issues are settled (meaning how long it will take for their office to draft an agreement and divorce papers, as well as how long courts take to process the papers once they are submitted). However, no attorney can look at a case at first blush without knowing if your spouse is going to fight with you and tell you in exact terms what to expect.

Additionally, the "How much?" question also comes with issues when trying to predict a final dollar amount. The quick answer—A LOT! You have heard all the rumors that divorce is expensive—but please know that they are all true. Divorce is a huge financial commitment, and no matter how rich you are, you do not want to give your money to attorneys. But the real answer is that the length of a case correlates with cost, as most attorneys bill on an hourly basis. There are some attorneys who may offer a flat fee for certain services, but be careful to ask them about what additional expenses could be incurred. While a flat fee might be offered when drafting uncontested divorce papers, this might not include the drafting of the separation agreement, for example, which is an essential part of the divorce papers. Also, ensure that you ask about court-filing fees if you are dealing with a flat-fee model.

YOUR LAWYER'S OFFICE
SHOULD BE A JUDGMENT-FREE ZONE

Clients often come into my office saying at an initial consultation, "I am really not this much of an asshole!" Don't worry about what an attorney thinks of you personally. All they are thinking about is your case—what is going to work for your family and how they are going to get you through this. The attorney's office is like a confessional. Everything comes out, and there is no judgment. If you feel intimidated or judged after meeting with an attorney, do not choose that person. No matter how good their reputation is, you will not be able to help them do their job.

Your lawyer needs to make you feel comfortable and secure enough to say anything without feeling judged. Your attorney is not being hired to be your friend. He or she works for you and, in order to do the best job, needs to know everything about you without you using a filter and being nervous that if you say something wrong he/she will not like you. Don't be afraid to curse (if that is your normal way of speaking) or speak whatever is on your mind because you think it will offend your lawyer— trust me (I always say that my "virgin ears can handle it"), it's very likely that she or he has seen it all. The only thing to fear is that he or she will not have all the information necessary to properly represent you.

And you need to be clear with your attorney too at the initial consultation and during the divorce process as well. Be up front about your expectations. If you want a phone call after every meeting with your husband's lawyer, let your attorney know. If you do not like to be bothered and just need the high-level points, tell your lawyer that too. Attorneys are not mind readers. Some of my clients want an all-inclusive email summarizing every single detail of every meeting. Others would be furious with me for wasting their time (read: their money) with such communication. Feel free to change your expectations, too. You may want to know everything in the beginning, but once the lawyer gains your trust and you feel like things are under control, then you can step back from the details a bit. But being communicative about your needs and expectations is key to a working client/attorney relationship.

WARNING SIGNS—BEWARE

Do not hire this attorney if any of these issues occur during your initial consultation:

- The attorney agrees with every single position you take—no questions asked.

- The attorney spends more time telling you war stories than talking about your case.

- The attorney is rude to you in the initial consultation or is distracted and checks emails or takes calls when you are discussing your situation.

- The attorney does not take one note during the consultation.

- The attorney promises you that he/she can get you an outcome.

- The attorney tells you exactly how long this will take and how much it will cost.

- The attorney is either über aggressive (assuming that is not what you are looking for) or overly passive (assuming that is not what you are looking for). Remember Blake and the obnoxious and aggressive attorney who saved her marriage for a few years?

- The attorney gives you the "hard sell," and you can tell he/she is hungry and just wants your case because the rent bill is due.

- The attorney stares at your chest the entire meeting and/or says anything sexually inappropriate (jokingly or not).

- The attorney tells you the name and/or details of another person's case (if he does it to them, he will do it to you).

Choosing your divorce attorney is going to be the second most vital step (after deciding you definitely want to get divorced). You need to be strategic in your selection, considering process choice, expertise, location, cost, and psychological fit. But most significant is finding an attorney you feel comfortable telling anything to. Do your research. Planning ahead and educating yourself gives you the peace of mind required to make important decisions. Making smart choices can mean a stable, safe, and happy life for you and your children long after the divorce is over.

CHOOSING A DIVORCE LAWYER

- Comfort level
- Specialty
- Word of mouth
- Internet reviews
- Peer recognition
- Associates/partners
- Location
- Solo practitioner versus firm
- Soldier versus adviser

TEN SIGNS YOU SHOULD CONSIDER SWITCHING ATTORNEYS

As I said in the beginning of this chapter, you may not choose the right attorney on the first shot. Here are some tells that you may need to switch attorneys during your divorce:

1. **If your attorney is unresponsive.** Matrimonial attorneys are notorious for not returning calls and/or emails. This is unacceptable and you should not excuse it. This does not mean that if someone does not respond in five minutes you send a dismissal letter, but calls and emails should be returned within twenty-four to forty-eight hours from when you send them (extended for weekends/holidays).

2. **If your attorney is unprepared.** If you have a court appearance, settlement meeting, or even a scheduled call, your attorney should be on top of the details of your case and ready to go. If he/she does not remember you have children or forgets other crucial details of your case, that could be a sign that your attorneys are not tuned in enough to your case and you should find someone else who is.

3. **Your attorney does not regularly send you bills.** Your attorney is obligated to send you bills on a regular basis, and if he/she does not do so and is vague about how he/she is spending time (and thus your money), that could be a bad sign.

4. **Your attorney misses meetings or court appearances.** That is inexcusable (unless there is a legitimate life-threatening excuse)—"I forgot" does not do it.

5. **Your attorney misrepresents your positions.** If you want a schedule with your children that has you with them more than 50 percent of the time and then your attorney stands up in court and says, "My client agrees to shared fifty-fifty parenting time," then your attorney is not listening to you.

6. **Your attorney is disrespectful to you.** There may be occasions that your attorney could be frustrated that you refuse to abide by his/her advice and you may do things that are disruptive to your

case that makes things more difficult, but your attorney should not be mean to you. Your attorney needs to be able to always treat you with a professional courtesy.

7. <u>Your attorney disappears.</u> Your attorney is entitled to go on vacation (but should tell you in advance), and that is fine. But if he says that he "just has to go away for a while" and assures you everything will be fine, it won't be. (This happens, and if it's rehab, offer your lawyer your empathy, but please step away from the partnership.)

8. <u>Your attorney acts in an unprofessional manner.</u> You may be okay with your attorney throwing a full-fledged temper tantrum in front of your husband's attorney or the judge if you feel it is effective, but if that is not how you want to be represented, you should consider looking elsewhere.

9. <u>Your attorney does not have the promised experience.</u> Sometimes it is hard to predict in the beginning of a case whether a case will go to litigation or how involved it will be for the purposes of custody or financial litigation. So you may have an attorney who thought he/she could handle it when you first met but as the case progressed is now in over his/her head. That happens and is fine as long as that attorney recognizes that he/she is drowning and brings in either an expert litigator or financial expert to assist with the case. You do not want to be anyone's guinea pig.

10. <u>Your attorney is inappropriate with you.</u> This one may go without saying, but it is interesting to note that the Code of Professional Responsibility for matrimonial attorneys specifically states that matrimonial attorneys are not permitted to have sex with their clients. As you can imagine, the relationship you establish with your divorce attorney can be very close, as you are sharing secrets that your best friends do not know. You also have someone

who feels like your "hero" rescuing you from your horrid marriage. Feelings can be confusing, and you are in a vulnerable state, and it is the job of your attorney to not allow the lines to blur.

There is a reason that there are so many divorce lawyer jokes out there. There are people with questionable moral character who have law degrees and practice matrimonial law. However, there are also a lot of good lawyers and good people who are in the matrimonial field as well. Find an attorney who you can tell cares about you, your case, and your family and is not using your case to pay for their summer home. Trust your gut as to whether the attorney you interview is the right fit for you and your case. This person is going to play a very important role in your life during this difficult time—so choose wisely.

SECRET #7

Neither of You Are
as Wealthy as You Thought

Money, if it does not bring you happiness,
will at least help you be miserable in comfort.
—HELEN GURLEY BROWN

Everyone needs money, and most people like money. Yet women are "money-hungry whores" if women acknowledge that they want money (the joke of that is: a whore is just a business-savvy slut). Well, I am here to tell you that it is fine (even encouraged) to want money, need money, and even talk about money—especially when you are going through a divorce.

I understand that the last thing you may want to think about when your marriage is ending—you feel your children are suffering, and you are an emotional wreck—is finances. I hear you when you say that you purposely avoided that subject in college and are not looking to learn it now. While I do not mean to sound unsympathetic, you must understand that post-divorce you are no longer going to have the luxury of living in the financial dark and just relying on your spouse to make sure that the money stuff is taken care of. When you divorce, finances need to become part of your repertoire and you need to get ready.

FINANCIAL DIVORCE 101

There are four financial "buckets" in a divorce: (1) asset distribution, (2) spousal support, (3) child support, and (4) extra child-related expenses. While I go into depth on these topics later, the basic definitions are:

- Asset distribution: how your assets are divided

- Spousal support (a.k.a. "alimony" or "maintenance"): when the lower-earning spouse may receive financial support from the other

- Child support: how much support the primary caretaker will receive for the support of the children

- Extra child-related expenses: these are payments made to third parties on behalf of the children that are not covered in the basic child-support payments (e.g., Sienna's ballet class; Brody's swimming lessons). In some states, this bucket can sometimes be merged into the child-support bucket.

With these financial buckets in mind, you must figure out—with the assistance of your attorney and/or a financial expert—how they will best be filled.

WHAT IS THE MARITAL PIE AND HOW BIG IS MY SLICE?

When figuring out what your net worth will look like post-divorce, you need to first determine which assets are to be divided (are they marital or separate?), figure out how they are valued, and then, the process for division between you and your soon-to-be ex can begin. I must set forth a big disclaimer here: the way assets are divided varies greatly from state to state and sometimes even from judge to judge. I will be speaking primarily in relation to the laws of the state of New York, so I urge, encourage, and beg you to discuss anything you read in this chapter with your attorney as it pertains to the laws of the state in which you live, prior to taking this information as the gospel truth and relying on it to settle your own case.

Before embarking upon dividing the marital pie, you need to know the ingredients that comprise said pie. Remember the financial discovery part of the process and how to figure out what assets exist. However, once you know what exists, you need to then determine which assets are subject to division between you and your spouse.

Generally speaking, assets and income accumulated during the marriage are deemed marital assets and subject to division upon divorce. Furthermore, assets that are either owned by one party prior to the marriage, inherited, gifted by a third party, or received as part of a personal injury award are considered separate property and (with some exceptions) not subject to division upon a divorce (at least in New York).

I must dispel a common belief held among those who did not go to law school. Many people believe that because an account is simply held in your name it belongs to you. This is not the case—at least not usually. If the money you put into that account is marital money, i.e., it comprises income earned during the marriage, then odds are it will be considered marital property and subject to division by the court irrespective of title. So you know how you held off buying that Chanel bag and opted to save the money instead? You now have to split the savings. It sucks and is unfair—I know.

One of the great questions often asked by law school students regarding marital versus separate assets is whether an engagement ring is considered a marital asset or not. The answer (at least in New York) is no. It is a conditional gift given by one person to another before they are married, on the condition that they actually walk down that aisle and kiss at the end. Therefore, once a couple says "I do," the ring is yours (even if you end up divorcing a month later). Feel free to hock it after the divorce and buy something fun! Now, when considering the wedding bands, that is a different story. The answer to the marital/separate question of whether a wedding ring is marital (at least in New York) is yes. The wedding ring is marital property because you are married once you exchange them. I cannot even count the number of disgruntled husband clients I have who bitched about the $100K they spent on the engagement ring (that "she insisted on") who are not generally appeased when I tell them that at least half of the $10K platinum band is credited back. I always tell my friends who are engagement-ring shopping to spend less on the engagement ring and more on the wedding band (perks of having a friend who is a divorce attorney).

We must then discuss what happens to gifts that are given during the marriage—for instance, the beautiful diamond earrings he got you for your tenth wedding anniversary. Are these considered marital assets or separate? Unfortunately for you, they are marital, so he can arguably ask for one of them back. Then, let's think about the gifts you might have given to yourself, e.g., the pair of Louboutin stilettos you purchased after you closed your first big deal at work. Yep, he can claim one of those red-soled babies and make you hop around on one foot. I once had a client—let's call her Nancy—who had well over $1.5 million in designer shoes and bags and jewelry, all gifts given during the marriage (usually after the husband was caught cheating), hence marital property. During the divorce, the husband refused to just let Nancy have her stuff without there being a financial credit against the amount that he was due to pay her under the settlement. While he was legally correct in his ask, given the circumstances upon which she was given many of these items (not to mention the resale value of worn shoes—even designer ones—is not great), she was not budging on this point. He kept talking about selling everything on eBay and splitting the profits equally (which was obviously said just to taunt her). Ultimately, he let the issue go, but only after tens of thousands of dollars of legal fees were spent (and he had his fun making her cry). To protect against this issue, I will often include language in prenuptial agreements that says interspousal gifts are the separate property of the recipient, so a birthday gift (or a guilt gift) is really a gift—and cannot be taken back later.

EVERY RULE HAS ITS EXCEPTIONS

In the legal world, there are oftentimes many exceptions to rules that may cause separate property assets to either become a marital property asset or at least have a marital property component to it. For example, if a premarital asset appreciated in value during the marriage due to the active efforts of either of the spouses, then that appreciation could be a marital asset. Take a brokerage account you had before you got married that had $1,000,000 in it. Assume that you or your spouse actively managed that account, meaning you made regular trades—bought and sold stocks, and did not work with an outside manager to do so. Due to your wise trading know-how, the account appreciated to $1,200,000 during your marriage. In this situation, your spouse can claim the $200,000 of appreciation is marital and that he wants a piece of it (even though the account was yours prior to the marriage and you were the one who did the trading). The theory here is that you expended "marital time" to make the assets grow (time you could have been spending on growing marital assets versus your separate property assets), so there is a marital credit due.

Let me provide another example of appreciation that may not be marital. Say that you owned a piece of artwork before the marriage that was worth two million dollars. That artwork simply sat on the wall of your marital home and you and your spouse stared at it together and occasionally dusted it off, but that was about it. Now assume the artist dies and the value shoots up to three million dollars. Assuming you did not kill the artist, you had nothing to do with the fact this piece of art appreciated. This would be considered passive appreciation, and the appreciation would remain your separate property.

Active and passive appreciation arguments are the cause of much litigation. Often, when real estate appreciates (especially in New York City), a battle ensues to determine whether the appreciation in the value of the apartment was due to the fact you renovated the bathrooms or simply because the New York City real estate market has increased as a whole. Also (as previously stated), when you have couples who manage their investments while also working with separate investment managers, there is considerable controversy related to determining whether increases were passive appreciation—because it was due to the efforts of the separate manager—or possibly active appreciation, because the increases were due to the fact you called your manager occasionally and asked him to buy Apple stock while ditching the BlackBerry stock. Many clients who used to boast to their spouses about how they were trading geniuses, would now claim that they know nothing about the stock market (what do all those pretty symbols mean?) and all the wise trades in their portfolio that grew the account by millions in appreciation was the brainchild of Jeremy, the financial adviser.

Divorcing spouses also often litigate about what it means when you have a separate property asset and you transfer it into joint names. For example, assume the husband comes into the marriage with a house and then after the parties are married for a while, the wife says, "I do not want to feel like a tenant in my own home. We are raising our children here, I take care of this house, and I pay bills on this house—I want this house to be in our joint names." Not an unreasonable request, right? Husband switches title to joint, and now, ten years later, the parties divorce. Did the husband gift 50 percent of the value of the house to the wife, or should there be a separate property credit for the value of the house at the time the title was changed or the value as of the date of the marriage? What about individuals who had cash on hand at the beginning of the marriage and put the funds into a house that was purchased jointly? Does that mean that their separate property money is now lost in the joint asset or is that person due a credit? Assume one spouse had $100,000 at the time of the marriage and put the money into a bank account that was held in joint names. However, the parties also put their wedding presents and their incomes into the account, to the tune of $400,000. Then, taking it a step further, they used this account to pay for the honeymoon and their general living expenses. At the time of the divorce, the account had $250,000 in it. Does this mean the person who put $100,000 in to begin with should get the first $100,000 and the remaining $150,000 should be divided? Or can the other spouse argue that the original $100,000 was spent on the honeymoon and dinners, but the remaining $250,000 is composed solely of their income and wedding gifts? Since money is fungible, there are arguments to be had. In the end though, courts are more likely to include something as marital, rather than separate—so the burden of proof is placed on the person claiming that property is separate.

Upshot: When you commingle your separate money with marital money, it may be hard to disentangle after years of common spending and pooled resources. But more to the point, it may not even end up mattering, because odds are you will be giving most of the money to your attorneys so they can argue about whether it is marital or not.

WHAT IS ALL OF THIS CRAP WORTH?

Now that you have figured out which assets are marital and subject to division, it is time to figure out how to value these assets. In many cases it is easy: the value of a bank account is simply the balance that exists at the time an action for divorce is commenced (but what if your spouse went on a crazy shopping spree a day before he filed?). But what about real estate? Or businesses? Or personal property? Or pensions? This is where it can become more complex.

Your attorney will most likely hire appraisers to figure out the value of these types of assets. However, the problem with appraisers is they will primarily base their values on how assets similar to the one that is being valued is sold on the open market. This can be accurate sometimes, but it can also be way off. For example, I had a client who merged three apartments into one large apartment in a very fancy building in New York City. There really were no comparable apartments like this one in a similar-type building that the appraiser could look to for financial comparison, and there were no recent sales in the current building. Therefore, while the appraiser did the best she could, the value she came up with was incredibly high. In this particular situation, my client's husband ended up purchasing my client's interest in the apartment for 50 percent of the high-appraised value and then, when the ex-husband went to sell the apartment a few years later, he barely cleared what he paid my client for her half share! The best way to determine value is to let the market decide with an actual sale. So if you have an asset appraised and you buy out your spouse's interest in the asset for that value, be sure you really want it, because an appraised value could be way off from what you would get when it is ultimately sold.

I would be remiss not to address the issue of business appraisals as well. These always make me very nervous (even more so when I am representing the business owner). Unless you have a very traditional business and can compare it to a recently sold business that is identical to yours, it is so hard to determine the value of a business with any accuracy. The concern I have for business owners is that when you are having your business appraised for the purpose of your divorce, you obviously want the appraiser to find the value to be as low as possible. You have to assume you are able to do that by explaining very persuasively the flaws in the business (you are a small pastry shop and Dunkin' Donuts just moved into town and is stealing your customers—or whatever sob story you tell). This would then (hopefully) bring the value in on the low side. Now, fast-forward a year or so, and you must sell your business because DD really is a strong competitor. In this situation, once you have an interested buyer, the first thing you are asked is, "Have you ever had this business appraised?" This is when you hem and haw and explain, "Well, yes, but you really cannot go by that because this was used only for a divorce when I was trying to lowball my spouse." Please forgive my sarcasm when I say I am sure that will go over well—and that this buyer will be itching to work with you.

While valuing assets is not always hard to do, it is not always very accurate. Appraisals and the like can also be very expensive, so you need to be aware of that as well. Sometimes people will agree to neutral appraisers, and other times everyone wants their own. Then it becomes a battle of the appraisers with a third party sometimes stepping in to settle things. Of course, the bills keep racking up through all of this. And the assets you are focused on dividing lessen with each passing day.

WHO GETS WHAT?

Now that we know what needs to be divided and its corresponding worth, how do we figure out who gets what? While some states are an automatic fifty-fifty division, others are not (e.g., New York is an equitable state, not an automatic equal state). Some states will divide certain assets equally, and others will not. For example, in New York, a court may decide to split all the real estate and bank accounts equally, but not do the same for business interests. Divorcing spouses will go to war about what percentage the non-titled spouse should receive of the business in a buy-out.*

Appreciation of separate property assets are not always equally divided either. Courts will consider each party's contribution to the marriage, whether they are financial or nonfinancial (such as taking care of the home and raising children). There are numerous factors a court will consider when determining how assets are to be divided, and the last one is the good ole catch-all of "Any other factor the court finds to be just and proper." This basically allows the court the discretion to divide the assets any way the judge pleases. Therefore, in states that do not mandate an immediate fifty-fifty split of assets, there is a huge opportunity for drawn-out (and expensive) litigation.

NOTHING WRONG WITH MAINTAINING SOME HEALTHY SUSPICION

When negotiating a financial settlement, it is possible that the terms are not exactly as they seem, so be wary. For instance, your spouse offers you 50 percent of the brokerage account with the caveat that he will pick the stocks. While it may look as if you received half the portfolio, in reality he gave you all the stocks that had embedded capital gains while he kept the funds with a higher basis. This means that if you both cashed out the account, you would need to pay more in taxes on your share and that means that he gets more cash than you do. Scenarios like this abound—you must be on the lookout for double dealings that appear okay on paper but in reality are the opposite.

Another area to watch out for: When your ex suggests you keep the

---

*While it can happen, I find that only in rare situations do spouses maintain an interest in the business. After all, who wants to be business partners with a person who hates your guts?

house because it is where you raised the children. Sure, it sounds like he is being a mensch, huh? Not so fast. He may be offering you the house because he knows that if it is decided that the house will be sold, he will be paying 50 percent of the closing costs, which would not necessarily happen if you simply buy out his interest. To spell this out further, say the house is worth $2,500,000 (no mortgage for ease of the example). If you sell the house while married, there will be closing costs (I usually estimate high at 10 percent, which includes broker's fees, legal fees, taxes, and staging fees for sale)—that is $250,000. So, if you sell the house together and split the fees, the net profit is $2,250,000 and you each walk away with $1,125,000. However, if you keep the house and buy him out—you are paying him $1,250,000 and then if you sell it two years later when your last kid goes to college, you absorb the full $250,000 in closing costs. Not such a mensch after all, huh?

Forgetting even the closing-costs issue, you need to also think about whether you can actually afford to keep the house. You need to factor in all the expenses associated with the house, not just the mortgage and real estate taxes. Consider whether the roof is going to need to be replaced in a few years or if you will be land-rich but not have cash in the bank. Another thought: Is the real estate market inflated at the moment? Yes, you need a place to live, and yes, moving is a huge pain in the ass. But don't buy things you cannot afford to keep. You must be smart about which assets you fight for and which you say, "Thanks, but no thanks."

In closing, I know you thought it would be easy to figure out the asset split—*You get this, and I get that, and we are done.* Sorry—rarely does that happen. It is only in the case where neither of you have any separate property claims, your assets are easy to value, all emotions are kept in check, and everyone agrees to split things equally that you can walk away relatively unscathed. In this situation, it could be a cake walk. However, if one of those criteria is not met, you could be in for a long and drawn-out fight about the division of assets.

ASK QUESTIONS

When dealing with the finances of a divorce, no matter how much it pains you, you need to face this reality with your eyes wide open and a readiness to ask the questions you are curious about. In truth, many non-monied clients enter my office and feel embarrassed about how little they know about the finances of their marriage. Queries often begin with, "I know this makes me sound stupid, but ..." No ... nothing makes you sound stupid. As the saying goes, "The only stupid question is the one not asked." Many clients, often the woman in a marriage, are worried about sounding financially unsophisticated—and because of this they pretend to understand and agree with what their attorney is saying just to avoid sounding dumb. (You are not dumb for not knowing things that you have not been exposed to. Are you dumb for not knowing how to do a heart transplant? No.)

I plead with you here. Do not let the patterns of your marriage dictate your divorce. If your ex made you feel like you were unable to understand money and that you did not have to think about it since he was the breadwinner and you were not supposed to *worry your pretty little head about it*—please know he was wrong. The money earned during the marriage (assuming no prenuptial agreement is in place) is your money too. You are entitled to know what your marriage's financial picture looks like. Do not avoid the financial conversation. I realize that complex financial statements and balance sheets might not be your forte, but not taking part in this process leads to regrets down the road post-settlement.

It is not necessary for you to get your MBA from Columbia in an effort to be adequately informed during your divorce. Simply be willing to educate yourself and ask questions of your legal and financial advisers. That is what they are there for.

This rule also applies to the spouse with the funds. I have had successful CEOs sit in my office who know their company's numbers forward and backward but have no idea what is spent each week on their family's groceries. Do not simply agree with your attorney when you are working out the financial picture of your marriage. If you do, there is the possibility of you being the person who agrees to pay whatever sum is requested just so you can get the divorce over with and get on with your life—and a year later you realize you cannot afford the deal you made.

HIGH-NET-WORTH DIVORCE: YOU STILL NEED TO PLAY THE GAME EVEN THOUGH THE RULES DO NOT APPLY

When it comes to money issues in divorce, the laws are drafted to target those with simple financial lives and to try to make it cost-efficient so parties do not have to spend tons of money on lawyers litigating in court. However, a high-net-worth divorce can present many issues that differ from divorces not involving the 1 percenters (or the .0001 percenters). The greater concern for those with significant incomes and/or assets is that there are fewer "rules" for courts to follow. Therefore, judges have a huge amount of discretion in deciding how to interpret these laws to apply to high-net-worth cases. It is like squeezing a square peg into a round hole. While it may seem like a high-net-worth divorce could be easier to settle because it is apparent no one is going to go hungry, you must also remember that when there is more to divide there can be more to fight about!

AT THE MERCY OF A JUDGE

An example of how high-net-worth cases do not fit into the current statutory paradigm is as follows: in New York, the statute that governs child support is (as of the date of this writing) only set to consider the parties' combined parental income up to $148,000 when applying the stated formula. If the combined parental income exceeds $148,000, then the court looks to numerous subjective factors to determine the appropriate amount of child support. When a client earns annual income in the millions, the statute is of little use to a court. Here is the scale we are talking about: while most New York families may not earn a collective income of $148,000 per year, for a high-net worth couple on the Upper East Side of Manhattan, $148,000 may be the budget for their staff of nannies! And honestly, it may be on the low side. When I am advising clients who fall into these income levels on what his or her child support obligation may be, it is very challenging, because a judge has a lot of latitude in going above the cap. Once a judge determines that the $148,000 is not appropriate, then the court will look to the child's "needs" to determine child support, and that is when the games begin. Does that child "need" to keep the vacation home in Aruba? Does the child "need" a private car service? Maybe yes—maybe no.

Of course, there are some cases that have been previously decided by other judges that deal with high-net-worth cases. The problem with attempting to apply previously determined case law is that most high-net-worth divorces settle out of court, and even those that are litigated to reach a decision often do not involve publicly broadcast terms. So there is a paucity of precedent to go by, though there are certainly some headline-making amounts:

- Billionaire casino-magnate Steve Wynn (remember when he put his elbow through a Picasso and barely blinked) married his ex-wife, Elaine, twice and the second divorce, while sealed, was reputed to be $1 billion.[1] (Wynn was reported to be worth $3 billion—Nevada is a community-property state, so it was probably a good deal for him.)

- Mel Gibson and his wife, Robyn, divorced in 2011 after thirty years of marriage and did not have a prenup, which meant half of the marital property went to Robyn, to the tune of $425 million.[2]

- Rupert Murdoch and Wendi Deng, his third wife, divorced in 2013—for undisclosed terms, of course. But we do know that she kept the $44 million apartment (which had undergone a $50 million renovation). Murdoch's divorce to his second wife, now Anna Murdoch Mann, reported the divorce had a $1.7 billion settlement—part of which was a guarantee that her children would have a lock on their shares of the Murdoch family trust, which controls 38 percent of Murdoch's business holdings.[3]

- Jeff Bezos and MacKenzie Bezos most recently had the record-breaker settlement thus far (and will probably keep that title for a while), which reportedly had MacKenzie walking away with $36 billion (but before you wonder who her attorney was, recognize that the estate was reportedly valued at $137 billion and they divorced in a community-property state).

Notice how all of these big cases were ultimately settled. When it comes to real courtroom decisions dealing with significant incomes and extraordinary lifestyles, judges can basically do whatever they want.

COMPLEXITY OF ASSETS

The other challenge for high-net-worth cases has to do with the complexity of the assets that are being divided. There are some people who have millions of dollars in cash sitting in a bank account (or filling a mattress)—but those are very rare. The problem with many high-net-worth cases is that many of the assets are typically illiquid (except for those with the fluffy mattresses). Typically, those that fall in the high-net-worth space hold complex assets, whether it be deferred compensation packages, brokerage accounts, private equity investments, real estate, carried interests, and/or other business interests. Some assets cannot be split, and therefore there are numerous valuations involved (as described earlier) that are often subjective and involve creative methods of payouts. Many of these assets have intricate tax consequences and other costs of liquidation. There could be other concerns when dividing assets, like in the Bezos case, it was imperative that Jeff maintain enough Amazon shares that he still had control of the company. A business owner who is dividing shares or equity interest in a company (as opposed to a buyout) may distribute shares but make them nonvoting shares so the business owner does not need to worry about his/her spouse vetoing a business move because he/she is pissed that the kids were brought home late last Wednesday night. Dividing up assets in most high-net-worth situations is not a simple "you take half the checking account, and I will take the other half" situation.

The other issue that comes into play in high-net-worth cases has to do with the way these complex assets are divided. Many states (like New York) are equitable states, not equal states. This means that you are not looking at an automatic fifty-fifty split of assets. Even in some of the cases that claim to do an equal division of assets, there may be different ways of valuing certain assets that do not make the split as easy as cutting it down the middle. For example, in New York, business interests are rarely divided equally, even if the rest of the assets are. The level of asset division can be different based on the nature of the asset.

Even issues such as who pays for counsel fees can be different in high-net-worth cases. Typically, the monied spouse would be responsible for the majority of the counsel fees. However, when the non-monied spouse is receiving significant assets, a court may very well say that the spouse can afford to pay his or her own legal fees. Courts balance the need for both spouses to have similar levels of legal representation with not having that need give the non-monied spouse carte blanche to pursue frivolous litigation to put pressure on the monied spouse to settle. Therefore (especially in high-net-worth cases), there is a view that spouses need to have "skin in the game" and pay their own counsel fees to keep excessive litigation in check.

In many high-net-worth cases, you need to also consider outside factors beyond the income and assets to be divided. Many people who fall into the high-net-worth space have great concerns about information being leaked about their businesses and also may be in the public eye with an image to protect. When dealing with celebrity clients, this becomes a huge factor in a divorce negotiation. It is even worse when you have one person who is a household name and the other who is not but who obviously wants to be and is willing to use the details of the parties' divorce to get there (Britney Spears and Kevin Federline, for example—did we know who he was before divorcing her?). If you are representing CEOs of public companies, it is often imperative the public not know that his or her marriage is in trouble—the combination of a gossip-hungry public and a juicy divorce could cause the stock to plummet. I am sure that was running through the heads of Elon Musk, the cofounder of PayPal and CEO of Tesla and SpaceX, when he was divorcing his wife, as well as Jeff Bezos, founder of Amazon, when he was divorcing his wife. They definitely handled things quietly and most likely had the settlement completed before the press (and stockholders) got hold of the divorce news. Controlling the news story is imperative when dealing with the divorces of powerful people who can affect the stock market. That is also when you need to factor in confidentiality agreements and manage how the media is provided its information. Look at how Tom Cruise was able to keep the details of all three of his divorces under wraps—I am sure Katie Holmes, Nicole Kidman, and Mimi Rogers all signed very tight confidentiality agreements. Divorces for these people do not typically have just the parties and divorce lawyers at the table. Divorces at this level will involve a team of people, which can include the agents, the public relations team, the marketing team, the tax lawyers, the accountants, the business attorneys, etc., who all have a vested interest in how the divorce is resolved and then how the settlement is explained to the public. It takes a village to divorce a high-publicity couple.

THE RIGHT ATTORNEY

The aforementioned factors are why it imperative the attorney selected in a high-net-worth divorce has knowledge of operating within the high-net-worth space so that their experience allows them to predict how a judge may rule and what pitfalls they need to avoid. You need someone who is fully familiar with the variations of complex financial assets, compensation packages, knows the appropriate valuations that need to be done, and has creativity when dividing up illiquid assets.

It is important to note that high incomes matter very little when it comes to child custody. The law is the same whether you earn $10,000 per year or $10,000,000 per year. Custody standards remain as the "best interest of the child," which we discuss more later. This dictates that the court will consider the same factors regardless of income levels or assets when determining who shall be awarded custody of the children.

Before going to court in a high-net-worth divorce, I always ask my client, "How much do you like to gamble?" Remember, anytime you enter a courtroom, you are gambling on the actions of a judge. There is an inherent risk (albeit an educated risk if you have a savvy attorney), and the outcomes can be as unpredictable as rolling the dice in a game of craps. You may get a judge who does not believe that it is necessary for your child to fly private to retain his/her lifestyle. On the other hand, you may encounter a judge who feels that if this child has never flown commercial, why start now? I remind clients that litigation is often a luxury few can afford, because no matter how much money you have, you do not want to spend hundreds of thousands of dollars—sometimes even millions—on lawyers' fees.

I would like to take a moment here and bring you back to Blake from the intro. If you recall, Blake was worried what her husband would "give" her of the assets. When I hear clients say this (which is quite often), it is like nails on a chalkboard to me. Let's be clear—he is not "giving" you anything. You also own these assets, so it is a question of what he is keep-ing *and* what you are keeping. What is happening is that the marital pie is being divided—but you are not being given a "gift." Please remember that. So no matter how much money you may or may not have, dividing up that money is rarely easy.

Your Support Awards May Not Actually Support You

The two most beautiful words in the English language are "check enclosed."
—DOROTHY PARKER

As discussed in the beginning of this book—times are changing and courts are becoming less and less financially supportive of women who sacrifice their career to be home with the children. Gone are the days of lifetime spousal support. Gone are the days of arguing that a woman (or man) cannot get back into the workforce just because he/she has not been working for the past fifteen years while raising children. Arguments can be made that the skill set that a woman hones when running a PTA Tricky Tray Fund-raiser is very valuable and transferrable to the workforce. Think of what attributes that can be listed on the résumé of this woman:

1. excellent multitasker;

2. can handle difficult personalities (you know how competitive other PTA moms can be);

3. can organize large events with multiple moving parts;

4. fund-raising;

5. marketing;

6. executive assistant work;

7. driving;

8. money management;

9. good with children; and

10. management skills.

Let's face it, the odds of a busy mother dealing with the after-school lives of three children in New York City and having the magical ability to be in three places at once is quite a hirable trait. And then think of how so many moms have the extra physical feature of having eyes in the back of their heads . . . how great would that be to have at the office?

The fact is, more women are in the workforce than ever before. Women's share of the workforce was 45 percent in 1988 and climbed to 46.8 percent by 2016.[1] There are 74.6 million women in the civilian labor force, and women own close to ten million businesses, resulting in $1.4 trillion in receipts.[2] The proportion of working-women with college degrees has quadrupled since 1970 at 11 percent,[3] jumping to 40 percent in 2016.[4] In 2016, more than 37 percent of lawyers were women, which is a significant increase when compared to fewer than one in ten in 1974.[5]

More and more businesses are recognizing that providing a work/life balance with flexible work schedules permits talented women to stay in the workforce but still be able to feel involved with their children's upbringing. So as more and more women enter the workforce and more and more fathers stay home to raise children, there has been talk around the office cooler that spousal support will one day be a thing of the past. You know how you decided that it was better to stay home with your kids rather than continue teaching because your husband said that your whole salary was going to the cost of a nanny? Well, if you could hit the rewind button, you may want to do that. However, as you are reading today (and not in ten years), all is not lost, because while spousal support awards are less than they used to be, they are still being awarded. That said, no matter what financial award you walk away with after your divorce, I greatly encourage you to look into developing or honing some type of skill set that can result in a paycheck. I have told my clients (and friends) to work at Starbucks if necessary to secure health insurance. So while I am not saying that you should start perfecting your foam macchiato after finishing this chapter, I want to make the point that courts are expecting women to be financially contributing to the household, and you should be preparing for the same thing. I have so many clients (and spouses of clients) who expect that between spousal and child support that he/she will be able to continue to live in the "lifestyle to which she/he has become accustomed." I am here to break the bad news—odds are against it. And my prediction is—by the time I revise the third edition of this book, I am predicting that "it ain't happening at all" (and I hate the word "ain't"). Mark my words—the days of spousal support awards are numbered.

SPOUSAL SUPPORT: YOUR SHOE-SHOPPING MONEY

But while spousal support is still around and definitely part of the financial divorce discussion (the second financial bucket) I want you to understand the basics and how it works. As previously stated, spousal support is the money that one spouse will pay to the other for his or her financial support post-divorce. Spousal support differs from child support, in that child support relates to payments made for the purposes of supporting the children of the marriage. As I have stated, spousal support is not an "automatic" type of payment—and not every case results in payments of this type of support. As a general rule, cases that qualify for spousal support are ones where one spouse earns significantly more than the other spouse—and the lower-earning spouse needs to receive money from the higher earner in order to get to a point where that spouse can earn enough him/herself to be self-sufficient. Now, that may sound simple, but when it comes to dealing with spousal support in a divorce negotiation or trial, it is usually quite tricky.

A brief history and overview

Years ago, only women received spousal support and only in situations where they did not cheat on their husbands. In 1979 the case of *Orr. v. Orr* deemed it unconstitutional to award spousal support only to women. A study in 2010 stated that only 3 percent of four hundred thousand people receiving spousal support payments were men.[6] That was almost a decade ago, and while I could not locate any stats, a more recent study of sixteen hundred matrimonial attorneys stated that 45 percent of them have seen a rise in the number of women who are paying their husband spousal support.[7]

Now, I want to take a minute to speak about women paying men spousal support. I cannot think of one female client I have ever had who willingly agreed to pay her husband spousal support. Why? Because most of my female clients who outearn their husbands feel that they have still been doing the lion's share of everything and the idea that they have to pay their husbands one dime in support makes them livid. I can specifically think of a female client—let's call her Maggie—whose husband was a high earner during the marriage until he lost his job on Wall Street in the market crash of 2008. Maggie was working part-time during the marriage but earning a respectable salary that maintained their New York City lifestyle when added to her husband's income. Once he lost his job, he assured her he would find something else, but every job offer he received was "beneath him" and he kept turning them down.

Meanwhile, Maggie increased her work hours to full-time to supplement the lost income and her parents kicked in to help out with the private-school tuition. At first Maggie was very supportive of her husband finding the right job and was accepting when he turned down jobs because she did not want him to "settle." After about a year, his interviews became less and less frequent, and the job offers (even the bad ones) decreased significantly (but interestingly, his video-gaming skills increased). Now, all this time, Maggie was working her ass off and being promoted in her job and earning more and more money. And all this time, while her husband was home (not working), they still kept their full-time nanny because the theory was that he would have a job soon and they wanted to maintain consistency for the children (and it is very hard to find a good nanny in New York City—Maggie called her nanny her "wife" and said she could not have done it all without her because even though her husband was not working, he was not picking up much slack with the children in his spare time). Fast-forward another two years and husband is still not employed but now he is depressed (and he gained a ton of weight from sitting on the couch all day stoned, playing video games and munching). So now we have a husband who is grossly overweight, unemployed, and depressed. He was also angry because he felt that Maggie was not supportive enough of him, and he was obnoxious and rude to her and was bitter that they were no longer having sex. (I know, I know—I felt the same annoyance that I am sure you are feeling now—this woman was working fourteen-hour days, filling five hours doing sugar-cube igloo projects for the kids and homework and running from soccer games to dance lessons and all the other "mom" stuff, so she was a selfish bitch using her last five hours of a day to sleep rather than blowing her depressed, mean-spirited slob of a husband.) Anyway, the joke of the whole thing is that he was the one who told her that the marriage was not working and that he wanted a divorce. So Maggie entered my office and I have to be the one to tell this woman that I understand how unfair it feels, but that she is going to be on the hook for paying this guy some spousal support. Maggie was pretty fair-skinned, so it really was noticeable when her entire face turned bright red with fury. She went on about how he should be a real man! She ranted about how he turned down jobs and how he was capable of earning income and that he has a driver's license and could drive an Uber (which I have heard judges say when someone says they cannot work, although in this case, if he was stoned all the time it was probably not the job for him). As much as everything she said was true, I had to add insult to injury and explain to her that if we went to court on this issue, not only would she still end up paying him something in support, she would probably have to pay part of his legal fees (as well as her own), only to lose. She was trapped and enraged. And I felt for her, I truly did. After my meeting with her, I went into my partner's office and went off about how wrong it felt to me (and obviously to Maggie) that she was going to be on the hook for spousal support for this deadbeat. And my partner looked at me and said, "Why is that so wrong? Would you be as angry if the gender roles were reversed?" I probably would not have been. I would still have felt badly for the payer spouse having to pay any money to an ungrateful person who is obnoxious, but I would not have been as angry.

Now, let's talk about today. More recently, I had a male client—let's call him Len—come in whose wife was a high earner in the financial field. My client also worked but was much more involved with the parties' twin boys and (according to him) was more the primary caretaker of the children because the wife traveled a ton and worked crazy hours. As we discussed the type of lifestyle these people shared, it was a no-brainer to me that this was a maintenance case. When I mentioned this to my client, he initially was taken aback and said, "I cannot take support from her. Not only would she never pay me, but I feel like it would be wrong." Not remembering my outrage years earlier when representing Maggie,

I remember feeling surprised to hear him say this. I reminded him that maintenance awards were gender-neutral and there was nothing wrong with a man receiving maintenance from a woman. The words rolled off my tongue, and I could see that my giving him the okay made him reconsider his machoism. While I do not know if Len's wife was given the same advice that I had to give Maggie or whether it was my great lawyering skills, Len ended up a with a sizable maintenance package that helped him be in the position to have a three-bedroom apartment in New York City, which made it easier for his children to enjoy being at his apartment (although I am not going to pretend that the three-bedroom apartment he rented (even with his support package) and the five-bedroom town house the wife kept were even comparable). I refer you back to secret #1—times are changing.

THE SPOUSAL SUPPORT LOGISTICS

So here comes the boring but important question—how does spousal support work? Let me begin with my general disclaimer: spousal support, even more than asset distribution and child support, differs significantly from state to state. In fact, spousal support terms can even be different from county to county in many cases. So it cannot be stressed enough that you must speak to your attorney about the specifics of your case when it comes to spousal support. Even if you live in New York State, you need to confirm whether the judge you are in front of has some leaning when it comes to awarding spousal support. In my experience, I find judges (especially in high-net-worth cases) hold the most discretion when awarding spousal support, which is why the amounts vary so greatly from one case to another.

So how does the process typically work by current standards? Well, all states consider a list of factors when determining whether a person is entitled to receive spousal support. Some states have formulas (like New York) and other states leave it all up to the courts to apply various subjective factors when determining if spousal support is appropriate, and if so, in what amount. The factors vary so much from state to state that it would take an entire book simply to lay them all out in their most basic forms. Therefore, think about it this way in summary: most courts will consider whether that person has the ability to earn enough income to support herself or himself and the standard of living the parties enjoyed while married. In cases where there is a clear primary caretaker of the children, courts may also deliberate on whether that person sacrificed a career in order to raise the children. And, of course, there is always "any other factor which the court shall expressly find to be just and proper" when determining spousal support. This is, again, why spousal support is such a crap shoot.

FINANCIAL FACTORS AND FORMULAS

If there is a formula used by your state, you should ask your attorney if it is mandatory for a court to follow—but rather more of a suggestion. It may not be a hard and fast rule because the formula does not make sense for a particular case or because the court has discretion to deviate—and they so often do. As of this writing, in New York the courts will only consider combined parental income up to $184,000 when calculating spousal support. After that amount, the formula does not apply, and the courts have full discretion to apply the numerous factors, which leads to significant litigation and makes the formula somewhat useless. If your income is below $184,000, then it is possible the formula could be helpful, but again, spousal support is ripe for litigation because you can argue against the formula being applicable based on the factors for deviation. So, bottom line, spousal support can be a source of litigation.

The way I suggest spousal support is approached is more pragmatic than formulaic. Practicing in New York City and with the high-income-earning clientele I work with, my clients almost always earn in excess of $184,000, so this is why I find that the formulas are not very helpful. As we discussed, in the beginning of a case both parties are expected to complete a statement of net worth where you (and your spouse) will list all assets, liabilities, income, and expenses. This is a key document in any divorce and the basis upon which a divorce settlement is often crafted. Be careful when filling this out, as you do not want to undercut your expenses, but you don't want to inflate them too much either that you lose credibility. I know for many people this is a difficult exercise. I often joke that when you walk out of your apartment in New York City and take a breath of fresh-ish air, it automatically costs you twenty bucks. So in this regard, when you are first thinking about divorcing, you need to start paying attention to what you are spending. Start jotting down notes about how much cash you pay out on a day-to-day basis for everything and use your credit card more often so there is a paper trail. As so many of my clients bitch about doing the exercise of figuring out their monthly expenses, I decided to do the exercise myself to figure out what the fuss was about. I must admit—it was a painful exercise—but also eye-opening. I was shocked by how much I spend on food, which is ironic because I am always on a diet!

CALCULATING EXPENSES: WHAT TO LOG

As you begin logging your expenses, here is a list of what I ask my clients to provide details on:

- Housing: mortgage, maintenance, rent, real estate taxes, renter's insurance, condominium charges, and apartment assessments.

- Utilities: gas, electric, cable, alarm, phones (be sure to include all cell phones), internet, and water.

- Food: groceries, take out, dining out, work lunches, alcohol, and entertainment costs.

- Clothing: clothing and shoes for you, clothing and shoes for your child(ren), dry cleaning, and accessories.

- Insurance: life, automobile, theft, liability, umbrella, medical, dental, disability, optical, worker's comp, and long-term care.

- Unreimbursed medical: medical, dental, optical, pharmaceutical, surgical/nursing/hospital, and psychotherapy.

- Household maintenance: repairs, painting, gardening/landscaping, sanitation/carting, snow removal, pool maintenance, and extermination.

- Household help: domestic (housekeeper), nanny/au pair, and babysitter.

- Automobile: lease or loan payments, gas and oil, repairs, car wash, parking, taxi/Uber, and tolls.

- Education costs: nursery and preschool, primary and secondary, college, religious instruction, school transportation, schoolbooks, lessons and supplies, school lunches, tutoring, school events, and children's activities.

- Recreational: vacations, movies/theater/ballet, music, recreation clubs and memberships, hobbies, health club, summer camp, birthday parties, and extracurricular activities.

- Income taxes: this is applicable if you pay estimated tax payments.

- Miscellaneous: beauty salon/barber/spa, toiletries/nonprescription drugs, books/magazines/newspapers, gifts to others, charitable contributions, religious organization dues, union and organization dues, commutation expenses, veterinarian/pet expenses, support for a previous spouse, support for a child outside the marriage, unreimbursed medical expenses, and safe-deposit-box fee.

- Other: here is where you track everything else you can think of that does not fall under the aforementioned categories.

You should reference your credit card statements, your receipts, and any notes that you have in order to figure out these numbers. I also have my clients focus on numbers for two time periods—during the marriage and then what is projected post-divorce. Yes, the court is considering the expenses incurred during the marriage, but from a settlement standpoint, it is also important for me to know what my client believes he or she will be spending once the divorce is over, so I can best figure out how much money will be needed. Another point: When you are creating these charts, try to break out the expenses for the children related to unreimbursed medical expenses, childcare, extracurricular activities and lessons, educational expenses, camp, etc. (collectively the "extra expenses") on a separate chart.

Now, once you have your full expense list done, you will take out the extra expenses listed that are directly related to the children, but not any expenses for the children that are related to food or clothing. So let us say your full monthly expense list comes to $25,000* per month. You will then subtract the items that are extra expenses for the children, as defined above (which we will say is $5,000 per month). This brings your number down to $20,000 per month. However, for this exercise, we will assume that you are paying 20 percent of the children's expenses, which means we need to add $1,000 ($5,000 x 20 percent = $1,000)

*This is a typical budget for many of my clients, but the methodology can apply regardless of your budget.

back into the total, so the budget is now $21,000. From here, we start to make other subtractions to see if you need spousal support. We first subtract the child support that you may be receiving—let's assume that you are going to receive $6,000 per month. Your budget is now down to $15,000 per month. We next subtract the income you may earn from working outside the home (after tax), which we will assume for this example is $8,000 posttax per month,* so your shortfall is now $7,000. Sometimes at this point, arguments will be made that there should be imputed income to any financial assets that are being received by the person requesting support. For example, if the payee of spousal support is receiving $2,000,000 in investable assets, the payer of support will want to impute a rate of return to those monies, which of course is always an argument among attorneys and financial advisers as to what is the appropriate rate of return. For the purposes of this exercise, we will impute a rate of return of 3 percent (nontaxable) on the $2,000,000 for $60,000 per year or $5,000 per month. So if you subtract $5,000 from the $7,000 shortfall, your request for spousal support would be $2,000 per month (after tax).

Now, one important point to note about spousal support is that while it used to be taxable to the recipient and deductible to the payer, it is no longer true, due to the tax law changes as of January 1, 2019. So now, spousal support payments are not deductible nor includable as taxable income. Therefore, the tax savings that was previously a perk of spousal support (assuming the payer and recipient were in different tax brackets) is now gone, which makes spousal support even more difficult to resolve.

---

*If you do not earn income but a court deems you having the ability to do so, that phantom income could be imputed to you for the purposes of this calculation as well as any calculation of child support.

HOW LONG DOES SUPPORT LAST?

Once you have figured out how much you will be receiving, you must then determine how long the support will be in effect. Here again is where some states have formulas and others do not. The court still has discretion in determining the length of the support, however, I do think the formulas can be a better guide in determining length than they are in determining amount. As of this writing, in New York State the guidelines say that if you are married from zero to fifteen years, then support will be 15 to 30 percent of the length of the marriage; if you are married for more than fifteen years, up to twenty, then support can be awarded for 30 to 40 percent of the length of the marriage. If you are married for more than twenty years, support can be awarded for 35 to 50 percent of the length of the marriage. To make sure you understand this correctly, you could be married for fourteen years and receive support for a period of as little as two years! This is a big shift from what used to be the rule of thumb, where it was half the length of the marriage, and another sign of the changing times in terms of how courts are viewing maintenance payments. It is definitely something to keep in mind when you are negotiating your divorce. But again, there is a series of factors the court may consider if there is deviation from the formulas.

Spousal support typically terminates upon death and typically (although not mandatory), will also terminate upon the recipient's remarriage or cohabitation with another romantic partner. The idea is that your spouse will pay spousal support to support you, not Pablo, the hot young guy from Venezuela who you are shacking up with.

TAKING CARE OF THE KIDS:
NEGOTIATING CHILD SUPPORT

While spousal support may be moving toward being a thing of the past, child support is definitely here to stay (third financial bucket). I must throw out the same disclaimer as I did previously, when discussing spousal support and asset distribution. Child support has specific rules and formulas in each state. If you do not live in New York (and even if you do), please use this information as a guide only to understand the basics about how child support works and which questions to ask of your attorney.

CHILD-SUPPORT BASICS

Firstly, if you do not have children, then you can move ahead to the next chapter—there is no child support to be paid. That is simple enough. (Of course, you can keep reading if you are curious and/or plan to have children in the future and divorce the father of those children one day.)

However, if you do have children, then the first step is to see if your children qualify to receive child support. The age of your child is the first determining factor. Some states dictate that child support is paid until the child reaches the age of eighteen, and other states use the age of twenty-one (such as in New York). Assuming you have a child under the age of eighteen, the question is whether you will be the payer or the payee.

In New York, it is deemed that the parent who spends more than 50 percent of the nights in a calendar year with the child is the recipient of child support. Now, if each parent spends equal time with the child, then the parent who earns more money pays child support. New York does not give credit for time spent with the child when calculating the support obligations, which is why child support can sometimes be a motivating factor when people are negotiating custody. Many other states do give proportional offset credits for time spent, so it is imperative you consult with your attorney to see if the numbers change based on the amount of time the higher-earning parent spends with the child.

Most states use a shared income model when calculating child support. This model is based on the concept that the child should (as close to possible) live the same lifestyle the child would have enjoyed had the parents remained together. Therefore, the child should receive the same proportion of parental income that would have been received if the parents had not separated. There are some states that use a percentage of the parental income model and others that use a totally different approach. Again, it is important to consult with your attorney.

To understand how most of the basic models work, consider the following:

- The income of the parents is added together to figure out the combined parental income.

- A formula is applied to the combined parental income. However, different states use different formulas. For example, in New York, the courts, at the time of this printing, apply their formulas only to the first $148,000 of combined parental income. This number increases based on the cost of living. Then, there are percentage amounts that are applied to the combined parental income based on the number of children: one child is 17 percent; two children is 25 percent; three children is 29 percent; four children is 31 percent, and more than five children is no less than 35 percent.

- The child support obligation is prorated between each parent based on his or her proportionate share of the total income. The payer's obligation is payable to the payee as child support, while the recipient of child support is retained and presumed to be spent directly on the child.

In this situation, let us consider an example. Assume, for easy math, one parent earns $60,000 and the other parent earns $40,000 and there are two children. The combined parental income would be $100,000 and the applicable percentage would be 25 percent. So the basic child support would be $25,000, which would be divided between the two parents, with the higher-earning parent paying 60 percent (or $15,000 per year) and the lower-earning parent being responsible for 40 percent ($10,000). Those funds would be used for the basic expenses associated with the children.

Now, what happens if the combined parental income is above the threshold amount? That is an excellent question. This is where things get interesting, because most states will then apply various factors to determine how much above the cap should be applied. If the combined parental income is around $150,000, it is not probably that big of a deal, but if the combined parental income is $1,000,000 a year or more, then it becomes a real battle with attorneys to figure what the court should award (see the previous chapter on high-net-worth divorces). It becomes a question of needs and lifestyle.

The most common complaint I hear from payers of child support is that the money is not going toward the children's expenses, because how expensive is it to buy the kids Kraft macaroni and cheese every night? What many people do not understand is that if the child primarily resides with one parent, there are millions of incidentals that are also paid for, in addition to food, clothing, and shelter, and these costs add up. However, there are also many cases where child support ends up being simply disguised as spousal support.

"THE EXTRAS"

In addition to basic child-support payments, there is also the last financial bucket of extra expenses, which are typically made to third parties on behalf of the children, related to education, health insurance, unreimbursed medical expenses, childcare (when the primary caretaker is working), and extracurricular expenses/camp.* So how are these paid for? In New York, these are typically paid on a prorated basis between the parents and are in addition to basic child support. I understand some other states include these types of expenses in basic child support, so you need to double-check how it is handled where you are located. You do not want to be in a situation where you are happy with your monthly lump-sum basic child-support amounts and then find out you have a ton of other expenses you must pay to third parties with those monies. Depending on what type of activities your children are interested in, add-on expenses can be costly, so you want to be very careful when negotiating these points. If you are divorcing when your children are young, you have no real idea about what type of activities they may be interested in when they get older. The last thing you want is to be in a situation where you agree to pay for all extracurricular activities and then find out your child has a proclivity to horseback riding and wants her own horse!

Please note that child support is nontaxable, which means the recipient does not need to pay taxes on the money received and the payer does not get to deduct the payments (same as spousal support). So this is typically difficult for the payer, as the support is largely calculated on gross income numbers (some minimal taxes are deducted in New York, and there may be more tax consideration in other states), but the payments are after tax. So, if you are in a 40 percent tax bracket and paying $36,000 per year in child support, you need to be earning around $60,000 per year from your job to pay your child support obligation. And this does not consider the payments you will be making to third parties for your child's extras

---

*I usually find that extras for a child's typical New York City lifestyle (e.g., private-school tuition, contributions to the private schools, nannies, car services, sleepaway camps, European and/or tropical vacations, sports lessons, dance lessons, tutoring, health insurance, therapy, etc.) is around $100,000 to $150,000 per year.

that are also subtracted from post-tax dollars. These factors need to be carefully considered and weighed when you are negotiating child support, and/or the terms of how extra expenses are going to be paid.

THE FORMULAS AND NEED FOR NEGOTIATION

While child support is usually formulaic in most states, there is still much negotiating to be done in most cases. Some basic pointers I would advise you to discuss with your attorney when negotiating child support are as follows:

- Even if you are in a state that has child support terminating at twenty-one, very often it is negotiated that child support will continue past the age of twenty-one, until the child graduates from college or reaches the age of twenty-two or twenty-three. This way child support is not pulled in Marcus's last semester of college.

- During the college years, many states will permit a reduction in child support for an amount equal to the room and board being paid for college, assuming the child is not living at home and the payer is paying for college. This avoids a double-dip payment for room and board.

- When negotiating what is considered to be educational expenses, you may want to think about and specify in your agreement that some or all of the following educational expenses are to include: (i) tuition; (ii) any required assessments or contributions (for which the payer shall be entitled to any permissible tax deduction); (iii) the cost of school trips and other similar expenses charged by the school; (iv) textbooks; (v) sports equipment and/or uniforms required by the school; (vi) teachers' holiday and end-of-the-year gifts; (vii) school supplies; (viii) school pictures;

(ix) transportation expenses for the child to and from school; (x) school uniforms; (xi) computer equipment; (xii) cell phone expenses for the child; (xiii) allowances; and (xiv) all tutoring expenses for the child.

- When negotiating what is to be considered for college expenses (assuming you include an obligation for college, which you can kick down the road if your child is very young and too far off from college), you may want to think about and specify in your agreement that some or all of the following college expenses are to include: (i) SATs and PSATs or similar college entrance examinations and preparatory courses for college; (ii) application fees to the schools; (iii) the expenses of trips to visit the schools; (iv) tuition; (v) room and board (including reasonable off-campus housing, including but not limited to rent, utilities, internet service, food and meal plan); (vi) books, laboratory, and other fees and items charged directly by the college or university (such as student activity and registration fees); (vii) computers, computer equipment, programs, and software reasonably required for college; (viii) fraternity or sorority dues; (ix) study abroad and work abroad programs; (x) back-to-school supplies and dorm room setup expenses; and (xi) up to four round-trips per school year (five, if the child attends a trimester school) by coach (or comparable) accommodation to and from the child's principal residence.

- When negotiating extracurricular expenses, you may want to consider and specify in your agreement that some or all of the following extracurricular expenses will include: music lessons and equipment; sports lessons and associated equipment and uniforms; driver's education classes; camp or summer activity tuition, transportation, uniforms, and equipment reasonably required for participation in said activity; teen tour or like summer activity.

You may also want to include in the extracurricular section which parent is to pay for any religious school, as well as any religious ceremonies (bar/bat mitzvahs, communions, etc.).

- When negotiating what is to be considered as unreimbursed medical expenses, you may want to think about and specify in your agreement that some or all of the unreimbursed medical expenses are to include: medical, dental, orthodontic, ophthalmic, therapeutic (including psychiatry, psychotherapy, other mental health therapy, physical therapy, social skills therapy, speech therapy, and occupational therapy), pharmaceutical needs, copayments, medical equipment, and prescription drug expenses.

- While this is not necessarily applied to child support, one thing to also consider and negotiate is who gets to claim any tax benefits associated with the child. This should be discussed with your attorney as well as your accountant.

- You want to make sure there are life insurance provisions in the agreement covering the payer's child support obligations and the insurance provisions name the payee as the beneficiary. This ensures that should the payer die, there are sufficient monies available to make the payments necessary for child support and the extra expenses.

- You should discuss whether you want your child support payments to be subject to a cost-of-living adjustment.

- If there is a childcare provision, you should specify at what age the childcare obligation terminates, meaning that you are not going to still be having a babysitter drive your sixteen-year-old child to her babysitting job.

I know the child-support part of your divorce was supposed to be easy because there are at least some formulas for the court to follow. This remains true if your income falls within the caps and your child does not incur many extra expenses. However, if your combined parental income does exceed the income cap considered by the state in which you live, and your child is involved in extracurricular activities, has medical needs, or attends expensive schools, there is still much to talk about. This shows just how important it is that you work with an attorney who is familiar with the ins and outs of how child support is managed in your state. Unlike any other financial component of divorce, this is not your money that you are talking about—but rather money for your child.

THE MONEY MARTYRS

When figuring out your budget it is imperative that you be sure not to lowball yourself. Women will often feel "badly" when they list that they want to spend money on vacations, clothing or manis/pedis/massages. Don't! Your needs do not shrink when you and your partner split (if anything they increase—therapy now twice a week!) Recall how we said it is okay to be a money-hungry whore (remember business-savvy slut)? Well, it is. If he is going to think you are a selfish bitch anyway, may as well have your nails look good. Be sure to be realistic about your expenses and do not undercut yourself.

To the same token, do not assume that he is as pathetically poor as he says he is. If I had to count how many of my investment banker husbands would tell me that they are going to be bankrupt tomorrow, I would need to borrow your fingers and toes. I do understand that when your income does fluctuate and bonuses are not guaranteed it feels very scary to commit to large support numbers for your spouse and children. Many of us have lived through the financial crisis, and it was not pretty.

So there is some legitimacy to some of these concerns. However, that does not mean that you should be the one who automatically cuts your budget and lifestyle based on his what-ifs. When I am representing the spouse who has fluctuating income I will often include formulas to address what happens if he/she has a bad year (and also how the support is recaptured if the next year is a good one). But do not just assume that there will always be bad years and then reduce your budget for support purposes accordingly.

One important thing I would like for you to take away from this book is: don't be a money martyr.

Fifty-Fifty Custody Is Becoming the Norm

Whenever I date a guy, I think, "Is this the man
I want my children to spend their weekends with?"
—RITA RUDNER

A female client—let's call her Michelle—walked into my office once and said, "I need to have full custody of my children." When I asked her what she thought that meant, she said, "Well, I am the mom so I should get custody and my ex can visit them. This is nonnegotiable. I need to have custody." During my consultation with her she must have used the word "custody" at least thirty times. However, when I tried to explain to her what "custody" really meant—she would not hear of it and just kept chanting, "I want custody! I want custody!"

If this were ten years ago, I would let Michelle have her tantrum and then tell her to relax—she will get "custody." But, now, I need to let her have her temper tantrum and when she is finished, I have to break the news to her that if her husband wants equal "custody," she may have a fight on her hands. No longer does it require a mom snorting cocaine off the Elmo plates for a dad to get equal custody. Remember Matthew from secret #1, who worked all the time but wanted fifty-fifty custody and the judge supported him? That is the new normal, and Michelle and the Michelles out there better get used to it.

All that said, what does "custody" even mean? I can pretty much guarantee that Michelle did not know when she was demanding it in my office, and the odds are her husband did not know either. "Custody" feels more like an emotional word than a legal one. People know they want it and are willing to go to war for it, but do not even really understand what "it" is. In this chapter, I will offer the basics of child custody so you can better understand what you may be fighting for.

WHAT IS CUSTODY?

There are two parts to custody—residential and legal. Residential custody relates to figuring out when your children will be sleeping under your roof and when they will be sleeping under their father's roof. Legal custody, in New York, is related to which parent will be making major decisions concerning the child. These major decisions usually pertain to medical, education, and religious issues.

Of course, children benefit when parenting decisions are made jointly by both parents—and there is a push for this with divorcing parents in many states. If the parents share similar values, this is probably not problematic. After all, if you are of the same religion, your children are healthy, and they attend public schools and are doing well, then there is usually little to worry about. In that situation, joint legal custody is common, and the court probably will not worry about arguments arising on big-ticket decisions. Of course, that is an easy picture to paint—but joint legal custody does not always work.

PROBLEMATIC CUSTODY SITUATIONS

If you believe there are areas of contention related to religion, medical decisions, or your child's education, then I encourage you to bring this up when you talk about legal decision-making with your attorney. If you are unsure if there are significant differences of opinion between you and your ex-to-be, then consider the following:

Religion

If you and your ex-to-be have different religious beliefs (or you are of different religions) and you two have not yet made decisions regarding your children and their religious upbringing, then religion can be problematic in a divorce. I see issues arise more when there are parents of different religions and very young children who have not yet been introduced to religion. Disagreement is common in this area, just as it is common for one spouse to go from mildly religious pre-divorce to hyper-religious during or post the divorce. Finding religion could spur your soon-to-be ex to want to incorporate his new beliefs into your child's life. Additionally, the idea that your soon-to-be ex will marry someone hailing from a different faith and introduce this new set of beliefs to your child must also be considered. How would you feel about either of these situations occurring? We have had cases in our office where this becomes an issue because one parent wants to keep a kosher home or a vegetarian home (for religious reasons) and the other parent loves cheeseburgers and wants to take the kid to McDonald's. I actually had a case once where the mother was a vegetarian and wanted to fight over whether their dog should have meat.

If this makes you upset, then terms for the introduction of religion(s) should be included in the parenting agreement. In this agreement, religious upbringing can be outlined alongside the types of rituals or events you want your child to be involved in. Now is the time to discuss baptisms, religious school, bar/bat mitzvahs, communions, and other religious practices that will be followed (including but not limited to any food restrictions), etc.

Education

There may be limited options related to your child's education, depending on where you live and your financial means. If private school is not an option and your child attends a good public school, then there is nothing to fight about. However, what if your child is going to be attending a private school, and there are questions about which school fits best based on curriculum or other factors? Do we select a school that specializes in the arts, or is it more important to have a strong academic focus?

In my line of work, many educational conflicts rear their ugly head when a child faces difficulties in school or there is talk of IEPs (individualized education programs) and/or extra tutoring/special classes. One parent may believe extra help would be beneficial where the other parent thinks that such a route "babies" the child or enables him. While the financial aspects of education are dealt with in support, it is naïve to think the person responsible for writing the checks for the expensive tutoring lessons does not sometimes feel that money is being wasted (I often hear complaints about how a college-educated soon-to-be ex is perfectly able to help their child with her second-grade math, as opposed to hiring a tutor who charges $150 per hour). Additionally, there are many parents who do not want their children to have IEPs because they feel their children are being "labeled." While one parent might believe extra help would benefit their child, the other parent might feel differently.

There is another issue to address too—the gifted or talented child. I had a case once where the parties' child was incredibly intelligent (this is not one of those "My kid is a genius because he knew what sound a cow made when he was ten months"), but really a genius. The mother wanted this child to be pulled from his regular classroom for extra sessions and take some classes with the older grades. The father disagreed with that and felt it would be too much pressure on the child and also did not want him to have social issues, since he would not be taking all of his classes with his peers. Mom said, "He is bored and missing opportunities to excel," and Dad said, "Let the kid be a kid." So this ended up being an issue the parties fought about. (As an aside, after much motion practice and tens of thousands of dollars of legal fees later, it was decided that he would only get pulled out for math classes with older grades and would take private tutoring classes after school to advance his other academic skills.)

Conflicts abound when children either show a penchant to be gifted or require extra help. Of course, if these issues have been dealt with in the past, decisions should already be in place. Or if you and your soon-to-be ex share a similar mind-set and agree to follow the school's direction, conflicts are less likely here. If this does not sound like the two of you, address education concerns and the specifics of the decision-making process now in the parenting agreement.

Medical

I used to say that if you have two parents who participate in and follow Western medicine, then there are usually not many medical decisions for a couple of ex-spouses to argue about. The majority of parents simply subscribe to the belief that they will do anything in their power to ensure their child remains happy and healthy. But—and this is a big but—there are now increasing levels of conflict about medical decisions because some parents have vastly different opinions on what actually keeps a kid happy and healthy.

The number of children who are diagnosed with ADD, ADHD, OCD, autism, depression, and other special needs and conditions is ever increasing. There has been a 42 percent increase in ADHD diagnoses in the past eight years.[1] With the rising number of cases, it is no wonder that it is becoming an issue of hot debate. The percentage of American children being treated for ADHD[2] with medication is 6.1%, yet disagreements arise when one parent believes the child should be placed in therapy and/or medicated and the other parent does not. One parent says, "I do not want my child to be zoned out all day," and the other states, "My child needs help focusing." I had a client years ago—let's call her Jane—who had a thirteen-year-old daughter who she said was truly suffering. She would tell me stories about how it would take her daughter up to four hours to do simple homework assignments. Her daughter would write a sentence, erase the sentence, and then rewrite it over and over again to the point that the erasing would cause holes in the paper and then she would need to start all over again. Jane took her daughter to a child psychiatrist, who recommended that she be medicated. Jane's ex-husband did not believe in medicating children and claimed that Jane was exaggerating and that it was Jane's fault because she was not being patient enough. Of course, he claimed that their daughter finished her homework in mere minutes when she was at his house. To add to this, the daughter would tell Dad she was fine when she was with him (so as not to disappoint him, said Jane) but say to Jane that she wanted medication (or "help," as she put it) when she was with Jane. Jane was so distraught, because she really believed her daughter needed this medication and felt herself to be at a stalemate on getting it for her because the parties had joint legal decision-making when it came to medical decisions and that meant that Jane's ex basically had veto power. The parties duked it out in court and finally the daughter told the attorney assigned to her that she wanted medication, so the judge (and ultimately the father) respected that and we settled the case and the daughter was medicated (and I understand now doing very well). Of course, this took months, and during that time the daughter was not medicated and was also caught in the middle of her parents' battle (which as you can imagine did wonders for her mental state).

The moral of the story here is that medical decisions can be a hotly contested area, and when medical disagreements rear their ugly head, you may be in for a nasty custody fight.

THE DECISION-MAKING PROCESS

Decisions can be made in a variety of ways. Consider the following options: one parent gets to make all decisions; both parents split decision-making, with one parent making certain decisions and the other parent making other decisions; or parents are required to make decisions together, just as they did during their marriage, and a tiebreaker can be used when applicable.

However, even if one parent is in charge of decision-making, this does not mean that a parent can make last-minute or major changes as to how the child is reared. You cannot email your ex on a Saturday night and say, "By the way, I switched Eric's school yesterday. He starts on Monday, and I will send you the address of the school in the morning." The parenting agreement will typically have language that states any decision that is made, for instance, about medical decisions, schooling, and the like, requires major consultation with the other parent and all ideas about the situation need to be heard and considered. Sometimes, this type of process also involves consultation from a third party, such as a school counselor before any decision is made. Then, if the parents still disagree, the parent who has the decision-making power will be able to make the final call.

Another option that courts use at times is called "spheres of authority." In this type of agreement, one parent will make decisions on one issue, such as medical, and the other parent will make decisions on another, such as schooling. Usually, this follows a line of reasoning that the parent who makes certain decisions is an expert in that area; maybe Mom is a doctor and Dad is a school principal. It may work for some people, but I am not a fan, mostly because there could be overlap experienced, so the responsibility for deciding is not clear. For instance, if Mom has final say on education and Dad has final say on religion, who makes the call on whether a child goes to a religious school?

The last decision-making method is the one where parents make decisions together. The question must be posed though: What happens if they do not agree? Often this is addressed in parenting agreements, and a mediator or a specialist in the area that is being debated is engaged, such as a pediatrician for medical issues to assist and weigh in.

Finally, if you cannot agree, you can take the issue to court. Then, a judge can make decisions for your child. This the most expensive option, and worse, you then are working with a third party who's maybe never met your child and is deciding what is best for him or her.

Of course, religion, medical, and education are not the only areas where disagreement can arise, and some parents will develop specific language in their parenting agreement on how to handle situations like tattoos, body piercing, participating in certain high risk sports (football and hockey are popular ones), expensive gifts, at what age a child is allowed to get a phone or to learn to drive and date, if they can travel to foreign countries, introduction to R-rated movies, and so on . . . you get the picture. I have even had a client once include terms for cutting a child's hair more than one inch without written consent!

RESIDENTIAL CUSTODY

As discussed, the reality is the days of fathers having such limited time with their children are set firmly in the past. Increasingly, fathers approach me with the request of wanting fifty-fifty time with the children—making the mothers they are divorcing freak out (poor Michelle).

Before I get into the logistics of creating a parenting access plan, I want to speak a bit about the psychology of this very delicate and tender negotiation related to where your children will sleep at night. I am going to use Michelle as the example of the mother who has historically been the primary caregiver of the children. While the father loves his children, he has simply not been as involved in their day-to-day routines. Furthermore, now that Michelle's ex realizes he is not going to be coming home to the same house his children are sleeping in every night, he is claiming he wants fifty-fifty custody because he: (a) realizes he now wants to be more involved in his children's lives; and/or (b) wants to hit Michelle where it hurts.

You recall from earlier Michelle's reaction to this whole scenario (temper tantrum). So, this is where I ask Michelle (and you if you relate) a question: Are you opposed to fifty-fifty time because you do not want him with your children that often, or are you opposed to fifty-fifty time because you do not want to be without your children that often?

If you are opposed to fifty-fifty time because of the former, then you need to figure out exactly what your concerns are about him spending time with his kids. Is it because he may feed them Doritos for dinner and load them up on sugar ten minutes before bedtime? Or is it because he is unlikely to help them get their homework done properly? Maybe it is because bedtime is more of a suggestion with him as opposed to a mandate? What if there is a more serious reason—could he be verbally or physically abusive toward the kids?

If you have concerns about your ex being inappropriate or abusive to your children, this is a matter that should be addressed with your attorney immediately. It is imperative you do this so you can figure out the different ways to deal with it—it is possible that any access your ex has with your children may have to be supervised by a third party. If the concerns are more of the nature of him not raising the children in a way you approve, that is still a valid concern, but will not require supervision of his parenting access.

Any issue you may be internalizing or worried about should be raised with your lawyer, however, depending on the nature of the concern, there may be little you can do about it. It might be possible to draft language in the agreement that requires both parties to follow the same rules in each other's homes, however, rarely do such stipulations have any "teeth" to them. After all, what are you going to do if your son's bedtime is 9:00 p.m. but he does not go to bed until 9:30 p.m. when he is with your ex? Honestly, nothing—there is not a thing you can do here. While you understand that the half hour of extra sleep can be all the difference between you having your child returned to you as a sweet little boy or a sleep-deprived monster, odds are the court is not going to care. So feel free to include all the happy language you want in the agreement, but do not be misled into thinking it will actually mandate your ex to follow all rules. You need to be able to recognize the difference between concerns about appropriate parenting and micromanaging the time your ex is with the kids.

If your concern is more focused on your child not being with you fifty percent of the time, then you need to skip ahead to secret #12, which highlights the perks of divorce. I do not mean to make light of the fact you will no longer witness every move your child makes during his or her formative years, but I do want you to know that having your child with your ex is not the end of the world either.

Most mom-clients I work with are fine with their ex being with their children. However, this does not apply to their ex's being with the children 50 percent of the time, because that is not what has historically occurred during the marriage, and it is too much separation for the children (and for Mom). That may sound perfectly normal and reasonable to me and a judge, but your ex may view things differently.

The way I approach clients who regularly chant "I want fifty-fifty, I want fifty-fifty" is to ask them to forget about percentages for a minute and complete a simple exercise with me. I ask that they record basic parenting schedules in fourteen-day blocks. I will sketch something like this out for my clients on a Post-it:

M	T	W	TH	F	S	S
M	T	W	TH	F	S	S

From there, we begin talking about weekends, as it is this time period that is usually the easiest to figure out. Most couples (though not all—there are exceptions) alternate weekends with their children. In this regard, you will need to figure out what defines a weekend. Is it Friday to Sunday, Friday to Monday, Saturday to Sunday, or Saturday to Monday? Some people opt to break up the weekend (i.e., one person has Saturdays and the other takes over on Sundays). I generally advise against this because I personally believe it can be important to have your own uninterrupted weekend with your children as they get older.

Of course, if you and your ex are on good enough terms to have flexibility and divide and conquer (on Saturday, he takes Jake to soccer practice and you take Elena to a birthday party) all the better. But if you are not at that stage, then having a full weekend may be something you treasure, and it may also be easier for the children. Odds are if you have teenagers, they are going out with their friends on Friday night and sleeping all day on Saturday. Obviously, you need to do what is best for your family, but you should consider the different stages of your child's life, what their activities are, and what is important to you when deciding how you want to divide the weekends.

Once the weekend is settled (in this situation, let us say you are comfortable with Dad being with the kids on Friday after school through Monday morning), then I make an X on the Post-it note below the overnights Dad will be with the children (alternating Friday, Saturday, and Sunday nights):

M	T	W	TH	F	S	S
				X	X	X
M	T	W	TH	F	S	S

At this point, he has three out of fourteen overnights within the two-week schedule. Next up is figuring out the midweek overnights.

Generally, people agree on Wednesday nights access here, since it serves to break up the week and there is usually a desire for consistency. Now, we add Wednesday overnights into the schedule, and he has five out of fourteen overnights scheduled.

M	T	W	TH	F	S	S
		✗		✗	✗	✗
M	T	W	TH	F	S	S
		✗				

You and your ex also probably want to avoid having your kids bounce back and forth between your homes—but you also do not want to go through a long period without seeing them either. While those two desires conflict, I will usually be able to address it by adding an additional overnight on the weeks there is no weekend access. Or, if that is not possible, it could be an option to schedule in dinners when there are available blocks of time, for instance, on the Monday that follows the other parent's weekend. In this regard, access can be increased by adding a Thursday overnight on the opposite week's Wednesday overnight and a Monday dinner (noted with a *D*) following the other parent's weekend, as shown below. Recognize here that a balance between the need for stability, frequency of contact, and parental relationship continuity must be established.

M	T	W	TH	F	S	S
D		✗		✗	✗	✗
M	T	W	TH	F	S	S
		✗	✗			

This is a six out of fourteen schedule with a dinner. If this is your schedule, let's examine how this looks for you. You will see your kids on Monday, Tuesday, Wednesday morning, Thursday, and Friday morning.

During week two, you will see the kids on Monday, Tuesday, Wednesday morning, Friday, Saturday, and Sunday. You see the children eleven of fourteen days in the two-week window.

As for Dad, during week one he will see the kids on Monday, Wednesday, and Thursday morning, as well as Friday, Saturday, and Sunday. The only time that he will not see them is on Tuesday. During week two, he will see them on Monday morning, Wednesday, Thursday, and Friday morning. He will not see them on Tuesday or the weekend. Physically speaking, he will see the kids ten of fourteen days.

If you are looking for a pure fifty-fifty split, some parents will alternate full weeks and give midweek dinner access to the other parent. This depends, however, on the age of your kids. Alternatively, some parents will have a schedule where Dad has every Monday and Tuesday, and Mom has every Wednesday and Thursday. Weekends (defined as Friday, Saturday, and Sunday) are alternated.

M	T	W	TH	F	S	S
✗	✗			✗	✗	✗
M	T	W	TH	F	S	S
✗	✗					

Sometimes equal time can also be worked out when one parent has more time during the school year, but then the other parent makes up for the time during breaks or the summer. There are numerous ways to arrange these schedules in a way that benefits all parties.

When you are working on a parental access schedule, everyone should try their best to be honest about what they really can do. If you know you have office meetings on Wednesday mornings, do not fight as hard to get Tuesday overnights. Be realistic in your scheduling because if you enter into a situation you cannot abide by, the people who end up being most disappointed when you cancel are your children.

After figuring out the ongoing weekday access, you need to divvy up school vacations and holidays. More often than not, parents will alternate the holidays based on even and odd years. Of course, if certain holidays are important to one parent vs. another (especially religious holidays when the ex-spouses are not of the same religion) then one parent may always get the Catholic holidays while the other may get the Jewish holidays. School vacations and summer breaks also need to be decided upon. Again, do not fight for half the school breaks, which can equate to four weeks of time with your kids, when you know you can take only two paid weeks off of work. Just be realistic in what your life looks like when making these schedules.

There are obviously many other ways to structure a parenting access schedule, so you need to do what is right for you and your family. I would simply recommend that everyone stay focused and not get caught up in the percentages. The realities of what will work best for your children, as well as for you and your ex, are key. The schedule that is considered "best" for your children is one both parents can stand behind.

Please note there are no parenting police that come to your house at night to make sure you and your ex are following the written custody agreement. If you and your ex want to work out some access schedule other than what is written in the agreement, you are free to do so. The parenting agreement is really only to be used if the two of you cannot agree on how access is to be handled. That said, even if you and your ex are in a very amicable place and seem to be on the same page when it comes to access to the children now, I still require that my clients have some parenting schedule written in the agreement. You never know what the future will hold and while I hope that everyone continues to play nicely, as your attorney, it is my job to live in your worst-case scenario and be prepared for it. You never know what a new spouse or girlfriend may bring to the mix, or how your ex may react if there is a new someone in your life. I would not want misplaced jealousy to bleed into how parenting access is handled and you not to have a clear access schedule to fall back on if communication breaks down.

Custody, by far, is one of the toughest aspects of a divorce. It cannot be treated like a business deal (such as the handling of the finances) because you are dealing with something so much more prized than money—your children's lives and happiness.

PLAYING NICELY IN THE PROVERBIAL SANDBOX

I often hear from my mommy clients, "Before this divorce action began, he did not even know where our kid's school was located. But now that we are divorcing, he is at every school party, every parent-teacher conference, every school play, and walking around flirting with the moms and acting like he owns the place. He is on my turf and he best back off!" This is the typical "Daddy come lately syndrome" and yes, it is annoying, no doubt. However, whether this will be short-lived or not, you need to learn how to play nicely with him in the proverbial sandbox.

It is a legal strategy

I know you think (and most likely you are correct) that the only reason for his sudden interest in the fourth-grade musical of *Annie* is because his attorney told him he better begin showing up if he wants a shot at fighting for fifty-fifty custody. This is true because it is definitely the advice I give to my daddy clients who claim they want more access but admit they have historically had little to no involvement with their children's school and extracurricular activities. In this regard, I tell them to cancel those business meetings and get to the baseball field instead. So odds are your soon-to-be ex is getting the same advice from his attorney.

Considering this truth, I need you to be prepared for a couple of different scenarios, because one of the following two things are going to happen: (1) the interest will fade as soon as the case is over and the novelty wears off and he will "back off of your turf," or (2) the interest will not fade and your children will have a more involved father. So for the purpose of this chapter, we should assume the interest has not faded and he realized what he was missing out on all of these years (by the way, your daughter made an *adorable* Annie) and now he has made adjustments in his life to be around more. Perfect timing! Right when you finally get divorced, now he is showing up *all* of the time. How do you handle it? The answer is simple—graciously.

While it is painful, it is also imperative for your children that you and your ex put on a good show for the public eye. You need to, at the very least, act civilly when in public together for your child's events. If you can bear it, act friendly. There are specific and strategic reasons for you to heed this advice.

I AM TELLING YOU THIS FOR YOUR OWN GOOD

To begin with, your children will be wildly embarrassed if you and your ex fight in public. It may be very tempting to start in on him about his late child-support payments or the fact that he allows your kids to stay up until all hours of the night when it is his weekend as you are sitting on the soccer field together—but seriously, resist. Now, you may say, "I would be happy to discuss this with him off-line, but he simply ignores my texts and emails on the subject and will not take my phone calls, so the only time I have him as a captive audience is when we are watching Sam at soccer." I hear you, I really do. I also recognize how frustrated you are and how annoyed you feel that he has the nerve to show up for the game when he did not have the courtesy to follow through with his parenting access last night, leaving you to have to answer Sam's constant questioning of "When is Daddy going to be here?" With all of that being said, the soccer field is not the place to duke this out. There are other parents there, and you do not want to become fodder for gossip. Now, you might not care if people are talking about you and your ex—but rather you do not want your marital mess to spill over to Sam and affect his potential friendships with the other kids on the team or how he interacts with his peers at school.

Additionally, there are reasons to put on a happy face at school events. If your children are in private school, this is especially true—but realize this might be applicable to public schools too. Ultimately, schools and their administrators do not want to deal with your marital drama. They do not want to get involved in courtroom battles, nor do they want you to use their auditorium or gymnasium as the place where you wage World War III. There is not a school official on the planet who desires being called in as witness to your case either. Private schools carry with them the ability to deny entry to your children if you and your soon-to-be ex are viewed as liabilities. But I have been told that some private schools are more inclined to accept a child of a divorced couple that gets along. Why? Because these individuals have parenting agreements that they are beholden to that dictate how things operate with their kids. Ultimately, these divorced families can be easier to work with when compared to parents who are still married but battling with each other behind closed doors.

PREPARATION FOR EX ENCOUNTERS IS KEY

I oftentimes advise my clients to prepare for events after the divorce where their ex is going to be present (although this can apply during the divorce as well). This involves making sure you know in advance if he is going to be there. Many clients will also set up ground rules that need to be followed at such events related to their behavior. For instance, maybe you and your ex can agree that you will be pleasant to each other and that it is necessary for the two of you to be seated on opposite sides of the room. Or consider stating that if there are grievances that need to be aired, then this verbalization takes place only during the last five minutes of the event and somewhere private. In rare cases, I have had clients agree they can text each other nasty comments during the events but need to put a smile on publicly (which feels like a TV show to me—imagine Mom and Dad standing next to each other laughing politely at the teacher's joke while texting furiously, "You are a bitch" and "Nice outfit, asshole"). Not necessarily my recommendation as to how to communicate, but it is better than screaming at each other in the school halls. The point here is know what is the best way for the two of you to operate—and then stick with that plan.

Many schools and other organizations will hold separate events for parents who really cannot be in the same room together. However, in this case, one parent always misses out. For example, some sleepaway camps will allow one parent to come on parent visiting day, and the other parent will visit the next day. So one of the parents does not get to experience all the fun, excitement, and hoopla of visiting day and the look on their child's face when she sees her mom or dad for the first time in weeks. You also risk your child being resentful of the fact that she will be pulled away from her bunk for that extra Saturday to hang out with the other parent. The same idea is present for Back to School Nights, plays, and recitals. It really is a shame for the parent that gets the sloppy seconds and misses significant childhood events because he or she could not be adult enough with the ex to fake it for a couple of hours. My advice is to figure out how to be in the presence of your ex for special times—you will be happier and so will your kids when you are able to enjoy shared events.

JUST BEHAVE, PLEASE

Another important point to note here is that while you should not be fighting with each other in front of your child, you should also not be fighting over your child. Do not make your kid a Ping-Pong ball that is being bounced back and forth between you and your ex as you compete to see your son's science experiment while your ex is trying to get a look at all his art projects. Your child is probably already stressed out because he is unsure if the two of you are going to be able to get through the night. Do not add to the pressure he is feeling as he tries to impress you both. It is your responsibility to alleviate his stress while also dealing with your angst about being around your ex in public. Act like an adult and do not make your kid have to parent and police both of you.

In closing, my best advice here is that you need to consistently prepare prior to attending events where your ex will be around. Talk with your therapist before, and make sure you set an appointment for right after the event. Or write that nasty email to him—but do not press send!—before the event so you can get all your frustrations out and you no longer crave to verbalize it in real time. Have your mommy friends ready to shoot him dirty looks when he walks by them and ask the janitor who has a crush on you to trip him with his mop (just joking). Do what you need to do to get through it, and do not let your ex needle you into behaving badly. Focus on your kid—and less on your ex.

DISNEY DAD: HOW TO COPE WHEN YOUR EX IS THE "FUN ONE"

Part of the reason your ex may have the power to torture you is he may be what I call a "Disney Dad." What is ironic about that is for anyone who has been to Disney World with children (and if you have been there without children, there are other books you should also be reading), you know that it is called "the Happiest Place on Earth." But who is so happy? The parents are yelling at the children, and the children are being yelled at. Even the characters are sitting in smelly, hot costumes. The only people who are happy at Disney are those cashing in on the

$25 light-up Mickey balloons they tempt your child with on your way out of the park so it bangs into your head the whole way home.

Do you ever feel like your ex is acting like the proverbial grand marshal of the parade at Disney World, fiercely entertaining and wooing your kids, while you are the one who is left pushing the stroller and carrying the diaper bag? If this sounds familiar, you might be dealing with a "Disney Dad"! Disney Dad is defined as the "fun parent" or the person who does not worry about the day-to-day grind and a trip to their house is like a visit to "the Happiest Place on Earth" for your kids.

One of the biggest complaints I receive from some of my mommy friends is that they are sick and tired of being the "boring parent" or the "mean parent" because they have to lay down the law and utter the words, "It is time to put away your iPhone and do your homework," or "Eat your broccoli or you do not get dessert." This is especially hard to stomach every time your kids return from a weekend with your ex-spouse. Immediately, all the "fun" they had comes spilling out in one endless stream of consciousness—and then there is seeing all of the great new things they were bought over the course of two days! They brag about how late they got to stay up, the fact they ate ice cream for breakfast, how Dad just let them see a questionable R-rated movie, and the fact that no one ever told them no.

Yes, it is infuriating. And while there might have been some "good cop and bad cop" played as parents while you were still married, it feels like throwing salt into an open wound as you manage a divorce or adjust to life post-split.

Hearing "Daddy is the greatest" and "Dad is so much more fun than you, Mom" is never easy. It sucks—plain and simple. Parenting with a Disney Dad can make life with your kids that much more challenging. However, I do want to paint a picture for you—and this entails looking at the situation from the perspective of the guy who is currently residing in his own proverbial Magic Kingdom.

A definite lack of fairy dust

It may appear your ex has set up shop in the Happiest Place on Earth and turned you into the villain, but think about it this way: he feels terrible about the fact he is not home when the kids go to bed each night and is incredibly focused on making up for that in any way he can. Now, realize that some of these feelings may be intensified and heightened if he is the one who was responsible for your split or who initiated the divorce.

I understand considering this perspective does not quell your anger and it certainly does not allow you to feel less annoyed when you have to be the parent instead of the really fun, and cool playmate he has decided to personify.

Think about this. It is always going to be easier to say yes instead of no. Additionally, it is a far more pleasant situation to spend time being happy and playing and generally having a good time as opposed to fighting and hashing out the details of why vegetables are an important part of a diet and why a set bedtime is better for everyone's sanity. Your ex has limited time with your children and may not be faced with the daily grind of parenting. And truth be told, it could be something he is missing, as well as something he took for granted during the time all of you were living under the same roof as a family.

Yes, you could say he is trying to overcompensate now—and it may very well be true. However, also realize that from your children's perspective, they are dealing with a new reality, too. Having someone shower you with presents every other weekend might offer a temporary "high" of sorts, and suddenly having a parent who seemingly goes above and beyond in the entertainment department could offer temporary fixes after parents separate. But there is a stark reality here. I can guarantee that while a forty-eight-hour all-inclusive trip to the Magic Kingdom is a lot of fun in the heat of the moment, when they are tired and done at the end of the day, they just want to fall asleep on Mommy.

HOW TO AVOID FEELING LIKE THE "RUNNER-UP"

This new dynamic in your life can be hard—and it can feel bad. I am quite sure you have thought, "Well, I could be 'Fun Mommy' if I only had to parent every other weekend, did not have to worry about homework getting done, and did not have to think about a million other responsibilities day in and day out." However, your life, right now, requires you to care about the minutiae—the stuff that is not fun.

You are the one who has to go to the parent-teacher conferences.

You are the parent tasked with overseeing homework duties.

You are responsible for making sure your child gets to his doctor's appointment on time and eats a healthy and well-balanced diet.

You have the capability—and responsibility—of saying no.

Competing with Disney Dad and coming in with a silver medal sucks. It hurts even more when you know that on some level your ex is doing all he can to form a connection and offer meaningful experiences with your children, and that your kids are desperately missing him and craving his attention as well.

However, you also are aware that if he did not fill the role of Disney Dad there could be a chance your children might not want to visit him or find reasons to get out of weekends with him. Yes, you might get some small level of satisfaction from having your daughter cling to your leg while she cries, "No, Mommy, I do not want to go with him—I want to stay with you! Please! I love you—not him!" the fact remains, that sort of dynamic is not good for any party involved . . .you, your ex, or your children.

Realize that your kids are the ones who need to emerge as the winners in the competition you currently have going with your ex. It is going to be hard, I know. And it will take every piece of your willpower not to freak out when your ex shows up an hour late for an important ballet recital while being quick to pull out a new iPad as a consolation prize, suddenly making him the hero (even though you are the one who has sat through every practice and dress rehearsal *ad nauseum*).

There are going to be times when you just want to scream.

REALITY TRUMPS FANTASY IN THE LONG RUN

I encourage you to take a deep breath and step back. Recognize that your child needs to have a father in her life who she believes loves her. She also needs to feel confident in his love—regardless of how he may show it and your level of approval with his methods. At the same time, I encourage you to think about your own role in your children's lives and what that means to them. Remind yourself that love cannot be bought, and that children understand when a parent is there to support them, nurture them, and comfort them. A great new iPad might be one thing—but it does not mean a lot when a little one is afraid of the dark and needs Mom's kisses and hugs to fall back asleep.

Learn how to cope better by creating a barrier and not worrying about what happens when your child is on Disney Dad's time. This might go against your most basic instincts as a parent, but for your own sanity, I encourage you to master this. Realize that you have control over your relationship with your children when they are on your parenting time. You are setting boundaries for your child, who on some level needs and appreciates them. Channel your energy and focus on that—it will ground you if you come to the conclusion that your ex is on the periphery of your child's mind when he is not physically around.

The Disney Dad persona is fleeting. It cannot stand the test of time. Yes, Disney World is a very fun place to visit, but at the end of the day, a child craves stability and consistency. As your child grows, they will develop an appreciation for the parent who got it done, day in and day out. They will admire the parent who took time out of their day to get them to soccer practices and ballet rehearsals; they will appreciate that you helped them with their homework and made them brush their teeth before bed. Take comfort in the thought that while a weekend vacation might be nice, there is no place like home.

TOO MUCH POPCORN—TRUSTING YOUR EX WITH PARENTING TIME

Especially when you are co-parenting with a Disney Dad, it is very difficult to learn how to let go and not worry about the fact you are not in control when your kids are spending time with your ex. It can be a challenge to develop the communication skills that allow you to perform "outreach" with your ex so both of you can ultimately be good parents. However, taking on the perspective that you have a business relationship, of sorts, can provide for a successful parenting partnership that will benefit your kids.

Consider this analogy as you examine your communication methods and co-parenting relationship with your ex. I often recall the first time my daughter went away to sleepaway camp. For those of you out there who choose not to send your children to one of these camps, you probably find yourself unaware of the "rules" associated with this endeavor. And there *are* rules!

Sleepaway camp requires parents to pay a pretty good amount of money in tuition (it is honestly similar to some state-school tuitions) for a seven-week program. However, this barely compares to the amount of money you have to spend on the ton of shit you need to buy to stock your kids up for that less-than-two-month time away from home. Think about it like going off to college and moving into a dorm—but multiply it by two!

In any case, I digress.

The other thing that must be mentioned about these camps is that you put your kid on a bus that then drives out into the wilderness somewhere. From that point, you are only able to visit your child once, and are allotted four ten-minute scheduled phone calls all summer long. Yes, you can email your child—but she is not permitted to email back.

Beyond the forty minutes of phone time, parents do get snail mail letters that typically consist of your child checking the box related to "The food is good/great/okay." Did I mention this communication is completed on the cute camp stationary you were required to spend twenty dollars on?

What's more, my worries were further intensified because at this point in my life as a mother I was still picking out my ten-year-old's clothing on a daily basis (just so I could picture what she looked like during the day—working mom's guilt, anyone?) and also brushing her hair after a shower (her hair is thick and can be difficult). I was essentially faced with the fact I went from overmothering to no mothering.

I had angst about the idea someone might be mean to her at camp. Or what would happen if she lost her favorite stuffed animal? What if she could not find the right shirt that went with her cute shorts outfit? The what-ifs were honestly endless and consumed my thoughts day in and day out.

Now, the reason I use this bitch-worthy analogy when describing a challenge of divorce is the overall feeling of not knowing what is going on with your kid, sleeping away from them, and the ensuing lack of communication that happens while they are away.

SEPARATION AND COMMUNICATION

In your divorce, and in my sleepaway-camp scenario, both of us have no real choice but to let go and trust that those who are tasked with caring for our children are doing their job and giving them an experience that turns out to be good for them. Just as I had to believe in the abilities of the camp counselors, you, too, need to trust that your ex will do a good job with your children. Moreover, you must believe that when your child spends time with their father, it is a good thing!

However, there is a difference here. While I was unable to communicate with my daughter while she was at camp, you must put a priority on establishing some level of communication with your ex during the time they spend parenting. There is no shame in asking for him to send a picture of your kid or ask that they call you daily. You do not have to be left in the dark—and you also do not have to live with the assumption that it is normal for your kid to go "off the grid" so to speak when they are with their father. Both you and your ex will benefit when you talk about your co-parenting, what is going on, and how your kids are doing. This back-and-forth will only benefit your children overall.

GET YOUR INNER CONTROL FREAK IN CHECK

I have a friend, who is also a mom, who happens to be divorced from a real asshole (but of course, she is my friend, so I have to agree with her contention that he is obviously an asshole). They do not have a positive relationship, on any level, and she barely speaks to him about anything, let alone their co-parenting responsibilities.

In any case, my friend drops her children off with her ex on his assigned weekends and then, she has her own sleepaway camp experience. She does not hear from her kids again until she picks them up from school on Monday afternoon. There is no information communicated with regard to what they did with their dad, what he fed them over the course of the weekend, or which friends they played with while in his company.

It is so bad that one time my friend took her kids to see the same movie their father had taken them to over the weekend, but the kids did not want to tell her because they were afraid it would upset her. Seriously! You need to communicate with your ex. Do not make your children sit through *Finding Dory* twice. It may pain you to reach out and establish a line of communication, but it is necessary to find a way to learn how to speak with him now that you are divorced. Even if you were not good co-parents when you were still a married couple, now is the time you must think about your kids and their relationships with the two of you.

COMMIT TO COOPERATION

It might make you want to punch a wall when you realize your ex did nothing but feed your kids popcorn and candy all weekend, or that he actually allowed them to play Fortnite until three o'clock in the morning. However, you need to keep it in perspective. Unless the kids are in serious physical jeopardy or suffering emotionally, in the scheme of things, you need to try to let some of these things go. Regardless of how he gets under your skin when you are unable to control what your kids are doing, know that effective co-parenting does not require the two of you to be friends. It does not even require you to like him in the least, but it does necessitate cooperation. My advice is to just worry about the kids—it is both of your jobs to turn them into productive and emotionally healthy adults.

I have compiled some tips you might want to use when developing a communication strategy with your ex. Hopefully, these will also help you deal with your inner control freak:

- Create a clear, consistent schedule and rules you can both abide by and both sign off on. Be careful not to dictate it to him—but rather agree on it together.

- Discuss any parenting-related developments, important issues, or changes with each other. Keep him in the loop on things relating to the children. Remember, even if he is not worthy of his "#1 Dad" mug, he still should know what his kids are up to.

- Develop a plan, including scheduling appointments, when the two of you must talk about a problem; always remember to be polite, but also firm, when working toward solutions. There are many programs and parent calendaring apps out there that can be helpful (My Family Wizard, for example).

- Realize that trust is important—and you have to prove that you are trustworthy too!

- Retain civility and be reasonable. Remember that both of you are only human and you are each trying your best in this new reality.

- Stay on topic. When you are talking about the kids, make the conversation just about the kids and do not take this as an opportunity to throw a few jabs in there about his younger slutty girlfriend.

Co-parenting can be a situation that is immensely harder to deal with than when your family was living under the same roof. Or, co-parenting can be easier now that you are living apart, by letting some of the control go. This new situation can be successful if you are both open to doing the hard work of communicating and finding a happy place where your kids thrive from both of your attention. You know your ex is not going to do everything your way, and vice versa. Both of you have to be okay with that, and so long as the doors of communication are open in relation to your children's welfare, there is a good chance you are on the right path. Welcome the idea that the two of you have valuable strengths to contribute to your children as individuals and as parents—*even if you know your way is better!*

PROMOTING TIME WITH DAD

There are many healthy and effective ways to cope with time away from your child, but first and foremost, you must realize this parenting time has to happen. Parental access is an important part of divorce. The court looks to you to facilitate the relationship with the other parent. It is one of the fundamental responsibilities of the primary parent. If you skip out on access time, the court could say that you are alienating the child and discouraging the relationship with the parent.

There is no need to feel guilty about urging your child to spend time with his or her father. Fostering the child's relationship with the father is essential. While you may feel your ex is a horrible person and an even worse parent, he is a parent. This man is your child's father, and you must allow the relationship to happen.

I get that a new custody arrangement may be hard for you and your children. But transition and change are all about attitude. Break free from the sadness and anger and discover how you can make your child's time away more enjoyable. If your ex is not a planner, then take it upon yourself to purchase tickets to the zoo for your ex and the kids (with his permission, of course). Pack fun projects, crafts, or games for the child to play with Dad. Time spent planning positive parenting time with Dad eases the adjustment and promotes an optimistic outlook.

ANY CRAYONS IN YOUR BAG?
ADJUSTING TO TIME AWAY FROM CHILDREN

Since you have now hopefully accepted that your ex is going to have the children at times, and that they will not die from the extra bag of M&M's he sneaks into their school lunches, you know your kids are going to be okay. But the question now becomes—will you?

Pacing the halls trying to adjust to the strange silence. Missing tucking your little one in at night. Waking up in the middle of the night wondering if she is safe. The first night spent away from your child can be the most difficult and painful part of divorce. Will you ever get used to her weekends away with your ex? How will you survive this unbearable parenting time without your kids?

Years ago, one of my favorite clients—let's call her Rachael—once called me from Starbucks in tears. She and her ex had fought like cats and dogs over every fifteen-minute increment of their parenting schedule— when their twin three-year-old girls would be with Mom and when they would be with Dad. As I heard her tears diluting her mochaccino, I realized it was the night of the girls' first overnight stay with their father. When Rachael eventually calmed down enough to speak, I asked her, "Do you have to go to the bathroom?"

"I guess I do. Why?"

"Well, you can just go," I said. "You do not have to maneuver your double stroller into the small bathroom, or struggle to position it so your children cannot reach the dirty walls. You do not have to make sure their beloved binkies stay off the urine-stained floors. You can just pick up your coffee and go!"

Silence on the other end.

"Do you have any crayons in your bag?" I asked.

She laughed.

One year after she was divorced, she called me, furious with her ex. "I am livid!" she said. "I need you to call his attorney and tell him to adhere to the parenting agreement. He is supposed to take the kids for two weeks. He knows I have a Hamptons house with my boyfriend and is just trying to screw up my plans!"

Can we take a moment to recognize the irony of this?

Change is hard, and the initial stages can be brutal. I recommend my clients go out with friends on the first night the children stay with

Dad. Go to a movie (something happy, please). Fill your schedule with minute-to-minute plans. Stay as busy as possible and in the company of others. The worst thing you can do is curl up on the child's bed and sob, soaking Poopsie, her favorite stuffed pig, with salty tears. Keeping busy and productive helps pass the time and allows you to pick up the child the next day with a smiling face and encouraging attitude.

Time away from your children is one of the hardest parts of divorce. But you will get through it. Almost all of my clients have difficulty at first, and almost all my clients end up anticipating the kids' visits with Dad and delighting in the newfound "me" time. Do some shopping, get a manicure, enjoy a massage, or hit the gym. Take whatever steps you need to let yourself be okay. Let yourself be you again, and not just "mommy." Before you know it, you are begging your ex to pick up your kids so you can board the airplane for a girls' week in St. Barts.

Your Children May Be Better Off after Your Divorce

Divorce isn't such a tragedy. A tragedy is staying together in an unhappy marriage, teaching your children the wrong things about love. Nobody ever died of divorce.
—JENNIFER WEINER

I would guess that probably 95 percent of the time clients walk into my office and say, "I really do not want to fuck up my kids with this divorce." (About 80 percent of them do not always word it that way, but they are all probably thinking it.)

I have also had many clients who walk into my office fresh from dropping their youngest child off at college and saying, "I made it! Time to divorce!" They feel they have sacrificed their happiness and freedom by staying in a loveless/unhealthy (maybe even abusive) marriage to "protect the kids." But when you think about it—what were you protecting them from? Being able to grow up watching their parents be happy? Being able to role model healthy relationships vs. living and suffering through an unhappy marriage? Did your children witness you be mistreated when they were young and impressionable? Is that what you want them to emulate in their own relationships?

Here is the big question: Is it better to have children raised in one unhappy home or in two happy homes? Obviously, you do not need a PhD in child psychology to know that it is better for children to grow up in one home with two happy parents. So we can solve that riddle right now. However, that is not what we are talking about here. We are talking about children who are growing up in a home with one (or possibly two) unhappy parents.

The studies do support that children who grow up with married parents are better off. But before you put this book away and say, "Forget it, I am not doing this to my kids"—you need to better understand why they say this and how that research relates to you and your children.

Kimberly Howard and Richard V. Reeves at the Center on Children and Families at the Brookings Institution recently conducted a study on *why* children of married couples do better.[1] They concluded that it could be more about the "parenting effect" rather than the fact that the parents are married. The parenting effect addresses the fact that parents who are married are more likely to have:

- Money: Married couples are more likely to be in a better financial position than a single parent. Remember how it costs more money to run two households than one? The more money, the better likelihood that the children will benefit from a better education, better medical care, healthier food, more extracurricular activities, more vacations and family time, etc.

- Time: Despite what you may feel your spouse actually does little to assist with raising your children, he is still part of the team (albeit maybe a weak link) so you can divide and conquer in a way that a single parent may not be able to do. A child who is raised by a single parent is less likely to get the attention that a child would if there are two parents in the home available to work on homework, drive to activities, listen to high school drama, etc. There are four ears, rather than two—it's simple math.

- Patience: The theory is that if you can deal with your husband— you can deal with your children. I say that tongue-in-cheek, but really the same skills that assist in maintaining a marriage—patience, commitment, a good sense of humor (I added that one in)—can also be skills that are important in parenting.

The analysis concluded that it may not be the "marriage" effect that helps children thrive but the "parenting effect."[2] So, what does this mean for you?

My takeaway from this study is that assuming money is not the issue (which I know is a big assumption), and you and your ex can remain engaged parents (remember that he is not disappearing here—just moving out of your constant eyesight) and you engage in plenty of yoga, therapy, and Xanax for patience (joking), then you can possibly maintain the parenting effect without having to maintain the marriage.

PROTECTING WHAT MATTERS MOST

There are things a parent can do to try to protect their children from the effects of divorce. One of the most important messages you can offer your child during their childhood (whether it be during a divorce or not) is that they will always have your unconditional love. If your child is secure and confident in the understanding they are loved by you and know that no matter what he or she does that your love is unwavering, they will be able to get through your divorce, as well as every other stage in life.

Here's a funny, personal story about unconditional love. It was during the Clinton/Lewinsky scandal back in the late 1990s that my mother called me at the office, which was a big no-no unless there was an emergency. I answered the phone—and honestly I was a bit annoyed by the distraction—to hear my mother say, "I just need to tell you something quick. If you ever had sex with the president, I would lie for you." I chuckled, feeling my annoyance pass, and said, "Duly noted," and ended the call. Her message was clear: unconditional love.

Children who are dealing with divorcing parents need to know that if they enjoy time with Dad, you will still love them. They also need to avoid feeling guilty when working to maintain the relationship with the man you no longer want to be married to. Children must know they are not being disloyal to you by loving their father. Give them permission to keep their dad in their lives and love him as if the marriage was still intact.

Additionally, children should not have to face choosing one parent over another. Oftentimes, a client will say, "Let my children choose who they want to spend Thanksgiving with." Frankly, this is a terrible idea—and will only end in tears, anger, and manipulation. Giving children this type of power is delivering the key to a manipulative kingdom (i.e., who gets me the best toys, gets me for the holiday). It can also cause great anxiety in children because, in essence, you are asking them to say who they would rather be with. Parents need to be the parents! By dictating which parent a child has to be with for the holidays, the child is given permission to go with the "bad" parent without feeling disloyal to the "good" parent.

DO NOT MAKE FRIENDS WITH YOUR CHILDREN

Learn this rule quickly. Your children are not your friends—nor should they be. Regardless of how old your kids may be, you should not be confiding in them, bitching to them, or offering them insight regarding your split from their father. Your children should not know the name of your lawyer or the judge, nor should they be privy to the details of any spousal support package you are receiving (or paying). Your kids, under no circumstances, should not have any idea about the child support that is being paid. Yes, I understand you may be dying to give them the details about why you are so infuriated with their dad, but resist the urge to speak. I also know you want your kids to know why their dad has left, however, they do not need to be aware of this specific information. Remember, children, no matter their age, never want to believe that their parents are bad or wicked people. Now, this may sound incredibly naive because they may already know the reality of your marriage's situation—but it is not your job to confirm their beliefs.

Do your best to keep your children out of your divorce on all levels—even in the areas you feel are no big deal. Do not pass messages to your soon-to-be ex through them (and realize that many parenting agreements have stipulations and rules regarding this) and never task them with being couriers of personal property. (Don't give them some old shorts left at the house that you are *pretty sure* are his.) Your children should simply live their life knowing that Mom and Dad love them, that they are provided for, and that they are allowed to be happy. It is true you are going to have to sacrifice your need for them to put on their "Team Mom" T-shirt, but I promise you, in the long run, taking the high road will be the best course of action.

I recognize how hard it is to keep your mouth shut during the divorce process. To leave your attorney's office after just receiving your husband's first ridiculous offer for settlement that would basically leave you a pauper and then have to turn to your five-year-old and put on your happy face is not easy. But to get angry in front of your child and when asked, "Why are you angry?" to say, "Because your father is a selfish bastard," does not help either. I am sure you can find a friend or two who are not your children who you can commiserate with—then, I invite you to bitch to your heart's content.

WHEN YOU "ACCIDENTALLY" BASH YOUR EX TO YOUR CHILD

I completely understand how you truly believe that your soon-to-be ex is the spawn of Satan. I also understand how much willpower it takes not to let everyone know how truly evil he is. However, in order for your kids to get through this period of their lives intact and healthy, you must exercise willpower and not speak badly of their father. Beyond this being simply horrific to hear if you are a child, it can also be detrimental to you in court if you are in the midst of custody litigation. One of the considerations a court takes into account when making custody determinations is whether the custodial parent will foster the relationship with the noncustodial parent. Alienation spits in the face of this—and can impact the party doing the trash talking. Here is a quick story—albeit not one of my cases. A mother alienated her daughter so badly from her father that the little girl would literally throw up at her father's feet every time she saw him. In this case, the court decided the alienation was so terrible that the mother lost custody. So now you have a child who is forced to live with a man who causes her to become physically ill at the mere sight of him. Who really loses in this scenario?

I get that everyone has a weak moment, and sometimes details of the divorce do get spilled to your children. Truth be told—it is a bad situation and something you really should avoid. That said, let's explore what could happen if you make it a point of bad-mouthing your ex to your child and try to get your child to hate her father as much as you do.

Option 1: Your kid could realize her father is an asshole and hate him for hurting you. She can then refuse to see him, and when she does, will act out and refuse to engage with him. It is possible she will grow up hating her father while she loves her mom. Now, I can see why that may seem like an acceptable option at the moment; your ex will be getting exactly what he deserves, after all. And it may be easy for you to feel he does not deserve your love or your daughter's affection. However, let us investigate this a little more. You have a child who still will probably have to go and visit her father, but now, she will have a miserable time—each and every time. Her happiness will be impacted. You also risk the possibility that she takes her anger out on you because you are supposed to be protecting her from this terrible man. You are now her protector, but she does not feel protected by you, and she feels vulnerable when she is with her dad because she hates him. Therefore, you know who she will end up feeling safe with? Her therapist. That is who she will spend hundreds of hours with on the couch as she deals with the emotional and mental shrapnel of your split.

Option 2: Your work is done and your child now hates her father. However, you are in a custody fight and it comes out to the judge that you have been involving your child in the divorce and telling her everything that is happening. As a result, she now cannot stand the sight of her father. The court gets involved and claims you have alienated your daughter against your ex. And trust me when I tell you the courts take this offense very seriously; so seriously, in fact, that you can lose custody of your daughter.

Option 3: Another way this could play out is that your child becomes very angry at you for bad-mouthing her father. She sees you as the strong one and him as the weak one, so she turns against you because she feels the need to protect him. Or alternatively, it backfires on you for another reason. As I stated previously, you are giving her unconditional love. She feels that no matter what she does, you will never leave her. However, because your ex left the house and your family's immediate day-to-day life, she may not feel such unconditional love from him. She thinks that if she is not nice to him, he may leave her, and therefore, she goes out of her way to be good to him and treats you like crap.

Question: *Which of these three options looks good to you?*
Answer: *None.*

The best way you can protect your children during a divorce is to keep them out of your divorce. They just want to be protected, safe, and to live in their happy-kid world. They do not want to visit your adult world, and you should not invite them into it. Do all in your power to create a united front with your ex and show your children that even though you are no longer spouses, you are still (and always will be) their loving parents.

AM I THE WORST PERSON IN THE WORLD? TELLING YOUR CHILDREN ABOUT YOUR DIVORCE

Few conversations are more gut-wrenching than having to inform your children that you and their dad no longer want to be married to each other. I have worked with many clients who have told me that looking their child in the eye and relaying this information has made them want to forget the whole divorce altogether. This conversation induces worrying about scarring your children for life, as well as fear over what their reaction will be. However, I do want to put your mind at ease. Children are more resilient than you think, and if you reassure them that it will be okay and make sure they understand that you and your ex love them no matter what, it is very likely they will emerge from this process intact. The important thing to remember is that it is your handling of this divorce process that will have the biggest impact on how they handle it.

Let's face it, children are narcissistic and are primarily concerned with their individual needs and desires. They are not yet in possession of the mental ability of seeing their parents as people—as unique humans and individuals who have dreams, goals, and wants. To your kids, you are simply Mom, and your soon-to-be ex is simply Dad. Being one of their parents is your sole identity, and that is in defense of *actual* children (admittedly, I know many forty-plus-year-old kids who are suffering from their own arrested development in this department). Your children do not understand that your life does not revolve solely around them.

Your child truly imagines that when you drop them off at the school bus and wave goodbye to them each morning, you actually stay in that same spot until they get off the bus after school in the afternoon. They cannot understand you have a life that does not directly involve them. Remember, their world is very small right now, why would yours be any different?

But it is because of this limited scope of understanding that it becomes very hard for them to process the idea that your relationship with their father is over. They do not understand the dynamics or complexity of an adult relationship; after all, how can you possibly fight and disagree if all you do is hang out by yourself at the bus stop all day?

YOUR KID IS NOT THE ONLY NARCISSIST

I need to be blunt and have you ask yourself if it is possible (even a little bit) that both you and your ex are also acting like self-absorbed narcissists. Of course, it would be totally natural if you were. It is very normal to develop some self-centered behavior during a divorce, even if you are trying to help your kids get through this hard time in your family. As a parent, you are well aware that your children's lives are changing dramatically, and you may even be in a state of angst as you witness their strife firsthand. However, you are also in a place of upheaval and spending a lot of time focusing on yourself and where it hurts. While it may be challenging to admit this to yourself, and I am betting you do not want to agree, but sometimes, you are just thinking about you and how you feel.

Despite your being focused on you, in your heart of hearts, you are worried about your children's coping abilities. The key to dealing with this requires you to consider their unique point of view. You must get down to their height level and consider the world from their childlike perspective. If your child is in therapy, I recommend you take some time to speak directly with the therapist prior to having the divorce talk. This health-care professional—who hopefully has a deep background in child psychology—might have a strategy and be able to coach you on how to approach the talk. This person may know some magic words and offer the help you need to get through this.

On the flip side, if your child is not in therapy, then this is something you may want to consider, as it can aid in managing the process. Alternatively, you and your child may also benefit if you consult with a child specialist regarding best practices on how to have this conversation. Different strategies could be applicable depending on the age of your child.

STAND UNITED—EVEN IF IN
REALITY YOU ARE ANYTHING BUT

One of the things you should avoid doing is telling your child about your pending divorce on your own. This is a time where you and your soon-to-be ex should stand united for the sake of your children—even if you cannot fucking stand him. Really, the only reason I can think of for this not to happen is if your soon-to-be ex has some rare and contagious disease that prevents you from sitting next to him. If this is not the case, you need to get over yourself and tell your kids together.

However, if you have requested this unity from your soon-to-be ex, and he refuses to be present for this talk, saying, "You created this mess and want to break up this family; you do it," then you need to script your dialogue in such a way that it is as if he is there in the room with you. Do not deliver blame in this conversation or show anger—no matter how furious you may be or how much you do not want your kids to look at you in a negative way. Resist the urge to say, "This is not my fault—it is Daddy's." Similarly, you should not say that this is your fault and not their father's. Blame and fault have no place in your conversation with your children because, at the end of the day, they do not care whose fault it is. Your word choice should remain reassuring, calm, and noninflammatory, and deliver the clear message that everything is going to be okay.

I am not trying to make light of this experience or how daunting it will be. It is indeed a lot to ask that you unite with your soon-to-be ex at this time and is even more difficult if he cheated on you, has decided he wants to leave you for the nanny and now has left you having to take the hit with him as you say to your kids, "Mommy and Daddy still love each other very much. But we also realize we are better people and parents if we are no longer living together."

Yes, I know, complete and utter bullshit.

WHAT YOU SHOULD SAY—AND HOW YOU SHOULD SAY IT

I wish there was a standard script I could offer here, but much of what you should say and how it should be delivered are based on your children's specific personalities and their ages. Age is an important factor when determining sensitivity levels and assessing how the divorce affects your life and theirs. Realize that your kids will demand some answers, and you should anticipate the possibility that they may ask the following questions:

- Will I have to move?

- Where will I live?

- How will time be split between Mom's and Dad's places?

- Whom will I live with, and do I get to choose?

- Will I be sleeping in a different bed every night?

- Where will I keep my toys and other stuff?

- Will I now get double presents on holidays?

- Will I get two birthday parties?

- Will my siblings live with me?

- What happens to my pet? Where will it live?

- Who will give me my allowance?

- Are you getting divorced because of me? Did I do something?

- Will you stop fighting now?

- Do you still love me?

- If I live with you, can I do whatever I want?

There could also be dozens more questions—or different variations on the queries mentioned. Furthermore, other questions that are more in-depth or based on emotions and real or imagined worries could also come up. But this could be dependent on what goes on inside your household and what your children might have witnessed. If there has been considerable marital strife, realize your children are probably aware of it and might have some questions about the mechanics of your marriage, as well as your divorce. This is where tough questions could be presented—and you need to be ready to answer them honestly. Ultimately, know that your children's greatest fear is going to be based on what is unknown about your split—and their imagination is probably envisioning a worst-case scenario. It is your job to quell their fears and make sure they know this is not their fault. Once again, remember their world is small, and it is easy for children to imagine that something they did wrong ultimately spurred this huge change in your household. (If Jon had not left his Rollerblades on the stairs, his father would not be leaving.) Work your hardest to make them know they are not to blame; you still love them, are dedicated to protecting them, and will always care for them; and through the plan you and your soon-to-be ex-spouse are developing, they will be okay.

WHEN SHOULD YOU HAVE "THE TALK"?

This is another subjective question and entirely dependent on what is happening in your particular situation. There is a significant debate among experts as to whether you should tell your kids as soon as you know you are divorcing or if you should wait until a parenting plan and some of the details about the future have been agreed upon with the help of lawyers.

I meet many parents who feel as if they are deceiving their children if they do not break the news as soon as the "D" word is dropped. Parents feel they are lying to their children if they have already been spending time at a lawyer's office and the marriage is definitely over but they are pretending things are fine. After all, what do you say if you are caught red-handed when your kid makes the observation, "Stacy's parents are divorced, and she says you and Dad act like her parents did before they got divorced. Are you guys getting divorced too?"

It is likely you are concerned that if you reply honestly, "Yes, Dad and I are getting divorced, but we are still fighting with lawyers about when you will be with me and how much time you get with your ass-hole father. So I do not know what is going to happen yet," then your kid is going to sit in his room freaking out because he thinks his entire world is about to explode. However, if you come out and lie, and say, "No, honey, all is fine with your dad and me," then your child is going to feel completely betrayed and blindsided when the truth comes out a few weeks down the road. And if you lie, your kid is going to remember and doubt everything else that comes out of your mouth as the divorce gets underway.

This is a tough call to make. Do you try to preserve the security of your children's world now? Or rip off the Band-Aid and get it over with? Whatever your course of action, it is best to do it correctly. Analyze your situation alongside the maturity level of your kids and their temperament. Either way, you and your soon-to-be ex should be focused on developing a parenting plan ASAP. This will help answer the questions your kids are sure to have and alleviate some of the uncertainty and fear they are experiencing.

It is easy to feel like the world's worst person right about now, but it is highly unlikely that is true (the world is filled with some pretty horrid people). Take a deep breath, formulate a plan, and approach this inevitable conversation with confidence and sensitivity. Be gentle and remember that presenting a united front with your soon-to-be ex is imperative.

TOP FIVE REASONS DIVORCE
CAN BE GOOD FOR CHILDREN

While I recognize claiming in any context that divorce can be good for children may feel like I am stretching, I want you to hear me out. In my research I came across many articles that would be helpful to any reader of this book who is questioning whether she is going to damage her child for life. These articles spoke about how divorce (as opposed to an unhealthy marriage) can actually have positive aspects for children. Divorce does not have to harm children. Here are some ways in which divorce can actually help children:

1. <u>The children do not see a loveless marriage as their role model.</u>
   If children grow up in a home where it is apparent that the parents don't love each other (and probably do not like each other) then they will believe that is what marriage should be. Think: do

you want your children to have the same type of marriage that you have? Monkey see, monkey do.

2. <u>Children may be able to have stronger relationships.</u> Many people believe children of divorce are more likely to repeat their parents' mistakes, but research shows this not to be the case. In fact, children who have witnessed toxic relationships firsthand are more likely to be able to spot warning signs before seriously considering a marriage. They're also more emotionally resilient and better able to build stable relationships later.[1]

3. <u>Children get one-on-one time with each of their parents.</u> I remember representing a woman client once—let's call her Robyn. Robyn had a thirteen-year-old daughter—let's call her Cate—and she was convinced that her soon-to-be ex-husband was not going to be able to parent Cate during his time with her because (as she put it), "He has barely said five consecutive words to her since she was three" (an exaggeration, I am sure). She believed that Cate would sit in a room all weekend long, be on her phone and totally ignored by her father. I am sure that (whether on purpose or not) her anxiety about Cate being alone with her father was probably contagious to Cate. Lo and behold, the first weekend came when the teenager was due to be with her father. As you can imagine, Robyn received numerous texts from her daughter on Friday night complaining that she was "bored," Dad was "trying too hard," and that she wanted to come home. Therefore (as you can probably also imagine), I was getting numerous texts from Robyn on Friday night telling me what a horrible idea this was and she wanted to fight in court so her daughter would never have to go to her father's house again. By the time Saturday afternoon came, the texts were less frequent. By Sunday, there were no

texts at all (which also resulted in texts to me from Robyn saying, "What has he done to her that she is not texting me?"). When her daughter returned to Robyn on Monday after school and Robyn gently prodded, asking, "How was your weekend with your dad?" The first response was "Fine." However, when she gently prodded more, her daughter said, "Did you know Dad was in a band when he was in college?" (Of course Robyn knew—it was the main reason Cate existed.) Her daughter continued, "I did not know that. I think that is kinda cool. He said he is going to get me a guitar and is going to teach me how to play the next weekend I am there." When Robyn told me this story, she could not decide if she was relieved, happy, or annoyed. What I told her to take from this story is that because Robyn was not there to direct the conversation and buffer the awkwardness between Cate and her father, he had to figure out how to connect with his daughter. And he did. This is a good thing. Many times people become better parents after divorce because they have no other choice.

4. <u>Children do not have to live with their parents constantly fighting with each other.</u> One of the main reasons I wanted to practice this type of law is that I felt I would be in the position to try to protect children from the impact of divorce. I speak endlessly with my clients about how they should not fight with their spouse when their children are anywhere near earshot. I had a woman client once—let's call her Lauren—who did not heed that advice. She would fight constantly in front of her kids because, as she would tell me, "He is just such an asshole!" Well, when I was working with Lauren on her expenses, she mentioned something about how there are always new teenage fashions (thus explaining why she needed so much more money for her children's clothing) and her daughter was into this new fad of wearing leg warmers on her

arms. Now, while I am not calling myself a fashionista, I knew enough to know that was not a new fad. I told Lauren to check her daughter's arms when she got home. Sure enough, her daughter was cutting herself and admitted that it was because she could not stand the fighting anymore. I am not saying that your child will engage in self-harm if you yell in the house and do not divorce, but I am saying that it is very damaging to children to watch and hear their parents constantly fighting with each other.

5. <u>Children learn to be adaptable.</u> While having different rules and customs at one parent's house versus another parent's house can be confusing for some children, it can also teach children important lessons that there is not just one way to do everything. Exposure to different methods of parenting can be positive for children and they can be more receptive to other authority figures as well. If properly directed by the parents, children of divorce can adjust to new situations easier than children who have had less exposure to change.

Every kid wants their parents' story to end with "And they lived happily ever after." This is what children are taught from the very beginning. So now everyone wants their Prince Charming and white horse. Well, as we figure out when we grow up—Prince Charming does not exist. And for the children of divorce, they may get that lesson earlier than others—but it may be a good idea for children to have healthier (and more realistic) expectations of marriage.

Divorce does not have to define your family forever. At the end of the day, all divorcing parents hope their kids will have the chance to grow into happy people who are capable of managing their own lives, having their own successful relationships, and interacting with their families. Growing up in two peaceful functional homes can be better for children than growing up in one broken home.

SECRET #11

You May Be in an Abusive
Marriage and Not Even Know It

Knowing what must be done,
does away with fear.
—ROSA PARKS

In the HBO series *Big Little Lies*, the marriage of Celeste Wright (played by Nicole Kidman) and Perry Wright (played by Alexander Skarsgård) is an excellent demonstration of how abusive relationships abound in seemingly perfect marriages. Celeste is smart (she is a lawyer by training), beautiful, rich, poised, classy, and a wonderful mother of twin boys. Perry (to the outside world) is a handsome, successful, doting father, and husband. However, while the family portrait would sell photo frames by the dozen, things inside the home are not as picturesque. Every time Celeste tries to rebut Perry's control of her he expresses his anger by choking her, smacking her, pushing her, kicking her, punching her, etc. (you get the idea). I do recognize that it is just a TV show (but a pretty good guilty pleasure), but it resonates so well with me because I have represented the Celestes of the world (and the Perrys as well).

Many of the clients I see are wealthy, well-educated, and objectively successful people. It would never be assumed that someone of their pedigree would be in an abusive relationship. I have heard numerous clients deny being in an abusive relationship because "that does not happen to people 'like me.' " People who view themselves as "strong" or "successful" cannot also resonate being a victim of anything. But victims of domestic abuse can be doctors, lawyers, CEOs, CFOs, teachers, accountants, SAHMs—you name it. Abusive relationships do not discriminate against the rich, the educated, or the pretty. So I hate to burst the bubble—but anyone can be in an abusive relationship. You just may not know about most because some people are better at covering it up because they feel they have an image to protect.

When considering the concept of what it means to have an "abusive marriage" it is true you might imagine a black-eyed wife toting the excuse of having "run into a door" or a woman who wears long sleeves in the summer if only to cover the bruises on her arms. However, what many people do not realize is that abusive relationships can take many forms—whether it be physical, emotional, or financial. Abusive relationships are incredibly complex but stem primarily from someone's desire to control another person. If you believe that you are in an abusive marriage or are married to someone who is abusive toward your children, you need to get help immediately. If the assistance you receive does not rectify the situation, then you need to get out. ASAP.

THE SCARS OF PHYSICAL ABUSE

According to the National Coalition Against Domestic Violence nearly twenty people per minute are abused by an intimate partner and ten million people per year in the United States are physically assaulted by an intimate partner.[1] One in three women have experienced some form of physical violence by an intimate partner and one in four women have experienced severe physical violence by an intimate partner (beating, burning, strangling). Intimate partner violence accounts for 15 percent of all violent crime.[2] If there's a gun in the home during a domestic violence situation, the risk of homicide goes up 500 percent.[3] Think about these numbers and realize that if you are reading this chapter because you are either in an abusive relationship or think that you may be—you are not alone.

Most Lifetime Network movies involving an abusive relationship or marriage focus on physical abuse. And this trauma is often fairly objective in nature, e.g., smashing a vase on someone's head is physical abuse. Sometimes, but not always, physical abuse will leave marks on the body that can be used as evidence of the abuse (unlike emotional abuse, where scars are internal and not visibly evident). However, the mere threat of physical violence or intimidation can also be present. The offending spouse does not have to raise his hand against his wife or children to obtain the control he desires. It can be as simple as preventing the other person from leaving the room or throwing a vase against a wall. Their spouse is not the target, but the message is delivered. And it is scary.

I had a client—let's call her Claire—whose husband punched her in the stomach when she was first pregnant, punched her in her face with a closed fist, and pushed her down the stairs (claiming it was an "accident") during their first year of marriage. She came to see me right after their ten-year wedding anniversary. Claire's husband never hit her again after that first year. But he would get drunk and he would get angry. And instead of hitting her in his fits of rage, he would simply raise his arm with a closed fist and flinch at her, and since she was able to recall what had happened nine years ago, she would wince—just as if he were hitting her again. The mere gesture was enough to put her in a submissive state of fear.

Sometimes abusive situations seem innocuous enough—for instance, when he grabs your arm a bit too tight as you turn away from a conversation or when he insists on hugging you in a way that sends a clear message about his superior physical strength. The essential point is that you should not be physically intimidated by your partner. If you are, then you need to explain all this to your attorney (and/

or therapist) right away so that the professionals you are working with know how to best help you navigate your situation.

DENIAL CAN BE DANGEROUS

It is all too common for an individual to make excuses as to why a spouse is physically abusive. "He had a rough day at work." "I was being annoying and deserved it." "It only happens when he is drinking." "It was a one-time thing." Some people even convince themselves they like to be hit. Celeste and Perry typically have passionate, crazy sex after he strikes her, and so she practically convinces herself it is part of their foreplay. Women who are abused will justify their abuse by saying that they also hit their husbands, and so it is equal—it is not equal. The denial can be the scariest part because it stops people from getting help. Only 34 percent of people who are injured by their intimate partners seek medical help for their injuries.[4] Many of my clients do not report abuse because they fear how a report like that could impact the spouse's career. Would he lose his medical license if they know what he does to me at night? Will his boss fire him and/or his clients hate him? Why would I kill my golden goose for a few slaps here and there?

Then there are the abused clients who keep the dark secret because they too want the image of the perfect family to remain. They don't tell because they feel like if they say it out loud to a third person, then it makes it true. And they are embarrassed and ashamed. So, instead a spouse will hope that it will not happen again. And when it does happen again, she says, "I hope it will not happen again." And when it does happen again, she says, "I hope it will not happen again." And the pattern continues.

Another concern of victims of domestic abuse is that even if they did tell someone—who would believe them? After all, where are the marks? Where are the witnesses? If it was so bad, why didn't you call the police? He is such a pillar of society, he would never beat his wife. So, isn't it risky to make these accusations, not be believed and then have insult added to injury that she becomes the "bad one?" Then if there is a custody fight—how does that play out? The risk does not justify the reward for some people.

In anticipation of a custody fight or someone not believing you, it is important that you document the abuse as best you can. Whether it be pictures (that are dated) or preferably you speaking to a third party about the abuse when it is happening so there is someone to corroborate your story should you ever come forward. Obviously calling the police and having an official record made would be ideal. But the bottom line is, whether you do something with it or not, you should do what you can to have evidence.

Now, I can understand the many logical reasons why a person would stay in an abusive marriage and/or keep the abuse a secret. Even though I understand the justifications for it, I still will turn to my clients and ask them to ask themselves, "How would you feel if your children were being treated this way in their own marriage?" If the thought repulses you, answer me this—why should you be treated differently?

MONKEY SEE—MONKEY DO

Most of my clients say they stay in an abusive marriage for the same reason they stay in nonabusive but otherwise dysfunctional or unhappy marriages—"for the kids." However, in abusive marriages, it can be even more damaging for children for the parties to stay together. Yes, I know you will say that the children don't know what is going on because "he is very good about only hitting me in the bedroom when the kids are asleep." But come on, it is naive to think that your children have no idea what is going on. At the very least the children will sense your tension and fear. One in fifteen children are exposed to intimate-partner violence each year, and 90 percent are eyewitnesses to it.[5] A boy who sees his mother being abused is ten times more likely to abuse his female partner.[6] Remember, a cycle of abuse is perpetuated when children bear witness. Children who are exposed to domestic abuse of a parent are at higher risk for health problems as adults. These issues can range from substance abuse, obesity, cancer, and heart disease to depression and unintended early pregnancy.[7] So, are you really protecting your children by staying in an abusive marriage?

THE REALITY OF EMOTIONAL ABUSE

Emotionally abusive relationships can be cases that are difficult to understand, identify, and characterize. What is the difference between a spouse just being an asshole versus being an emotionally abusive person? (Sometimes there is no difference, as the umbrella of asshole is pretty big.) The best definition of emotional abuse I've been able to find is:

> Any abusive behavior that isn't physical, which may include verbal aggression, intimidation, manipulation, and humiliation, which most often unfolds as a pattern of behavior over time that aims to diminish another person's sense of identity, dignity and self-worth, and which often results in anxiety, depression, suicidal thoughts or behaviors, and post-traumatic stress disorder (PTSD).[8]

So what does that really mean? Like physical abuse, the goal of an emotionally abusive partner is to exert control and create a power imbalance. The Australian Institute of Family Studies[9] cited the work of James Garbarino in identifying the five behaviors that an emotionally abusive person may display to cause this imbalance:

1. **Rejection:** withholding affection or refusing to show affection

2. **Isolation:** preventing the person from participating in normal opportunities for social interaction

3. **Terrorizing:** threatening the person with some sort of punishment, or deliberately developing a climate of fear

4. **Ignoring:** being purposefully psychologically unavailable or failing to respond to the other person's behaviors

5. **Corrupting:** developing false social values in the other person that reinforce maladaptive behaviors, such as aggression, criminal acts or substance abuse.[10]

Here are some of the questions you need to ask yourself to do the asshole versus emotionally abusive test:

- Is he constantly yelling or screaming at you for no reason?

- Is he constantly criticizing your looks, what you say, or what you do?

- Does he mock you incessantly? Does he do it in front of people?

- Does he curse at you and/or call you names?

- Does he threaten you and/or your friends and family?

- Does he engage in character assignation of you? (Saying you are "always late" or "never right.")

- Is he constantly pushing your buttons just to enjoy watching you react? (Which you should stop doing by the way.)

- Does he belittle you and/or your interests?

- Does he say that he will hurt you or himself if you do not give in to his wants?

- Does he withhold affection or sex or communication if you do not give in?

- Does he access your phone, email, computer, etc., without your permission?

- Does he read your private communications?

- Is he patronizing?

- Is he overly sarcastic, knowing you do not like it?

- Does he diminish your accomplishments? ("It is only a successful PTA car wash, it is not like you cured cancer.")

- Is he constantly dismissive of you? (Eye rolling, obnoxious smirks, exasperated sighs when you speak, etc.)

- Does he try to isolate you from your friends and family? ("I can tell your sister does not like me. Why would you want to spend time with someone who does not like your husband? Are you choosing her over me?")

- Does he constantly guilt you for wanting to have a life outside of him and/or your children? ("I just want to be with you because I love you so much, but if you would rather be with your friends, then I guess that is your choice.")

- Does he turn things around so his own bad actions become your fault? ("If you would have given me more blow jobs, I never would have had to go for that happy-ending massage.")

- Is he the master of gaslighting? Gaslighting is a manipulative method of control where he is able to mindfuck you into questioning your own sanity and/or memory. He may tell you that you are "crazy" and the incident you accuse him of "never happened" (happens often with physical abuse) and that you must have "imagined it." Or he will simply have a very different version of the events and tells you that you are a revisionist of history. Someone who is good at gaslighting will make you start to question what year it is, and this self-doubt will make you feel more dependent on him.

If the majority of these questions were answered in the affirmative, you may be dealing with a situation where your husband is more than just an asshole but he is emotionally abusive. You need to really think about what you believe the motive is for him when he does/says these things to you. Is he doing it to hurt and control you? Or is it because he has no self-awareness as to the significance of his actions? Either way, it is not good.

That said, all hope is not automatically lost if you have a spouse who exhibits emotionally abusive behavior. For instance, I have represented many clients (female and male) who truly do not believe or understand that they are being emotionally abusive to their spouses. On more than one occasion, I have had clients say, "I do not hit her; I provide financial support; she has a roof over her head and a good life. What is she complaining about?" I have also seen situations where a husband will make a joke at his wife's expense, and while he is taking a small jab, he mostly believes he is being funny. Furthermore, a wife who feels that she is being emotionally abused may also be sensitive to her husband's comments because it is pointedly coming from him. For example, if I were to critique my friend's outfit, she may laugh or agree with me or even ask if she should have worn different shoes. However, if my friend's husband were to say the same thing, then she would feel like she is being attacked, he is being über critical and therefore is being emotionally abusive. Sometimes the messenger is the one who gets shot (in a proverbial sense, of course).

Emotional abuse is very subjective and is hard to quantify. What may be seen as emotionally abusive to one person may not be to another.

Sarcasm for example, can be biting to some and amusing to others. I know this woman whose husband calls her Blondie, which I would find demeaning because he is clearly indicating that he does not think she is intelligent. However, she finds it cute (maybe because she is not smart enough to know she is being insulted). The point being is that the standard cannot be what others would describe as emotional abuse but what you would. Even if you are a very sensitive person who may take comments out of context, your spouse needs to know that and understand that whatever his behaviors may be, you are experiencing them as emotionally abusive and he needs to stop it and/or the two of you need to seek professional help to address these issues.

FINANCIAL ABUSE:
EXERTING CONTROL THROUGH MONEY

Financial abuse branches off of emotional abuse—but it is often a behavior that is not recognized as abuse. This situation occurs when one person controls another by using money as the threat. While there are more women in the workplace than ever before, in the majority of households the husband is still the primary breadwinner. Thus, it is the husband who maintains financial control over the wife. When an individual has lack of access to financial resources, there might also be an absence of options about where she can go and what she can do when the going gets bad.

Examples of financial abuse include:

- When one spouse keeps the other spouse in the financial dark and will not allow full transparency regarding what the marital assets are. Often, the woman is the victim here, and she has no choice but to accept whatever it is her husband tells her about their finances. This is usually rationalized with "I take care of the money—you take care of the home." Or in more overtly abusive situations, it can be based on the idea of "You are too dumb to understand money or our complex finances, so go back to what you are good at—spending money."

- When an allowance is doled out to the other spouse. If the wife "behaves" (whether that means by keeping the house clean or being sexually available), she will get more money. If she does not, then the husband cuts her off. This is different from having a family that decides to live on a budget. It is more evident when one spouse will eat at fancy restaurants and wear designer clothing while the other spouse eats at McDonald's and wears clothing purchased at garage sales.

- One member of a relationship has to account to the other person for every dime that is spent. I had a case years ago where the husband made millions of dollars each year, but required his wife to account for every penny spent (without exaggeration). She had to show him receipts when she bought pencils for their son's school supplies.

- A spouse does not permit the other to go to work—or makes that person feel badly about wanting to work. Some men do not want their wives to earn an income (or possibly outearn them) because they feel like their value in the marriage would be lost. If a woman can earn the money, have the babies, and keep the house, what does she need a man for? This concern often keeps men from encouraging women to work. I had a case years ago where the wife—let's call her Bonnie—wanted to work and be financially independent, but Bonnie's husband told her that she should not work because he made enough money for the both of them. He went further to say that having a wife work was "embarrassing for him, as it showed he was not a real man" and he was "insulted and hurt" that she would ever want to do that to him. Bonnie's husband would also guilt Bonnie by telling her that she was a "bad mom" and "selfish" because she wanted to work outside of the home and not be home with her kids 24/7. What Bonnie now realized was that her husband really did not want her to earn her own money so she would be 100 percent dependent on him and that was a way to control her. However, I am not saying there is something wrong with making the decision to not work outside of the home and focus on raising children—but it must be the choice of the person who is faced with this situation, not the choice of the spouse.

- When a spouse steals money. This occurs most frequently when one spouse has premarital funds or money that has been inherited and the other spouse feels entitled to use that money for whatever he or she wants (and without consulting their partner). Whether you are married or not, if you take the assets of another person without permission, that is stealing—plain and simple.

Financial abuse is a tough behavior to identify because in many healthy marriages, there is one person who takes charge of the finances while the other focuses on other aspects of their lives—and that is fine if it works for both of them. Financial abuse does not occur in every situation, and there are rarely clear or divided lines. The abusive component enters when you have a spouse who wants to be involved with the finances and is denied the opportunity. Or it can occur when money becomes the controlling element in a marriage. Just because one partner goes to work and earns an income each day does not mean that it is his or her money alone. While one spouse may not always make financial contributions to the marriage, there are noneconomic factors to quantify. That is a hard lesson for the nonearner to understand and for the earner to learn. I will often correct this type of language when speaking to clients. For instance, a nonearning spouse will say, "Let's see how much he will agree to 'give me' from the marital assets." My reply is, "No, let's see how the marital assets will be divided. He is not 'giving you' anything—you earned it too!"

WOMEN CAN BE GUILTY TOO

Yes, it is true this book is primarily geared to female readers. However, it must be noted that women can also be guilty of being abusers in relationships. When a woman is physically abusive, most men are too embarrassed to tell anyone about it. However, when a wife is emotionally abusive or financially abusive, many men do not even notice it. One out of four men report experiencing some sort of coercive control by an intimate partner.[11] Therefore, if you are the abuser in the relationship, you need to be the one to recognize the reality of your behavior and figure out how to deal with it in a healthy way before it spirals out of control.

Domestic violence is not always about size, gender, or strength. It is about control and power. While stereotypes will usually paint a man as the aggressor, a woman has the potential to also initiate violence. Sometimes women will look to neutralize their size or strength disadvantage by using weapons, and men may be held back from retaliation by cultural prohibitions that look unkindly on using force on a woman, even in self-defense. Therefore, if a woman is the guilty party, her actions should not go unreported. Abuse in any form should never be accepted.

THE ABUSE OF CHILDREN

When physical abuse is present in a marriage, it often also impacts a couple's children. The percentage of intimate partners who are abusers and also abuse the children in the household is between 30-60%.[12] So, what should be done if your spouse is abusive to your children? Again, if it is outwardly and objective physical abuse, such as punching a child with a closed fist, the situation needs to be immediately addressed, and you need to notify your attorney ASAP. There should be zero tolerance for child abuse, and you owe it to your children to protect them from an abuser.

But what I often see as the issue in a marriage is the thin line between discipline and abuse. This is one of the reasons why it is important prior to having children to speak with your spouse about their child-rearing beliefs and get on the same page about discipline. If you have concerns about how your spouse disciplines your child and that is one of your fears when determining an access schedule, again, you must convey those concerns to your attorney before agreeing to a parenting access schedule that may put your child in danger.

YOU ARE IN AN ABUSIVE RELATIONSHIP. WHAT HAPPENS NEXT?

I understand that it is very easy for an attorney to sit across the desk from you and say, "Why don't you just leave?" I know it is not that simple. I get that you have concerns about money and about your children having a relationship with both parents. You want to maintain consistency in your children's lives and feel badly that you are making a big deal about this because the abuse did not happen every day. You are also terrified about the potential aftermath of confronting abuse or proceeding with a divorce. A great worry of clients who are in abusive relationships is, "What will happen if I tell my spouse that I want to get divorced and then I have to live in the same house with him until the divorce is finalized? The abuse could be worse than ever." This is a valid fear and is something that needs to be seriously considered when strategizing with your attorney about how to tell your spouse the marriage is over. In *Big*

Little Lies, Celeste rented another apartment, furnished it and stocked the fridge with food before leaving her husband so she could easily bring her children to a safe, warm, and welcoming environment (I recognize that is where reality and Hollywood may not jibe, because you need the funds, the ability to access those funds, and the wherewithal to really pull something like that off). I typically suggest having any difficult conversation in a public place, like a restaurant, and plan in advance for where you and your children will sleep that night. It would be ideal if you can have the conversation when your children are staying the night at a friend's house; that way, you do not have to go home with your soon-to-be ex and you do not have to worry about your children being around. If you are genuinely concerned for your safety, make plans to stay out of the house. You need to work out a plan with your attorney that first and foremost keeps you and your children safe.

Domestic abuse is truly scary and should not be taken lightly. However, you should not turn a blind eye to what is happening. Take steps to get help for yourself, your children, and your spouse. And remember, if you have children and are allowing them to watch you as you are abused, you are guilty of playing a part in what "acceptable" behavior may be. They are learning lessons about what is seemingly viewed as "okay"—and a cycle of abuse could be perpetuated. You owe it to yourself and your children to break the cycle.

There Are Perks to Divorce!

The question isn't who is going to let me;
it is who is going to stop me.
—AYN RAND

Even though I have been working as a matrimonial attorney for some time, I often find myself feeling a bit uncertain about how to give the news to a client when I receive the official divorce judgment. Is it appropriate to call my client and somberly inform her that her divorce is finalized? Or do I send the document over with a gag oversize key to handcuffs and a card that says, "Congrats! You are free!" Regardless of how the divorce was entered into, all clients react differently when they realize that it is finally over. Mixed feelings are common. There can be anger, relief, sadness, and even happiness and unadulterated joy! But regardless of the feelings that are experienced or what a client's initial reaction to the divorce decree may be, there is a simple truth present: The divorce is now an official part of the past, and it is time to embrace and welcome the future.

WHAT HAPPENS NEXT?

While I would love to say all the legal mumbo jumbo is part of your personal history, we are not totally there yet. During this divorce process, your divorce lawyer has become a GPS of sorts in your life, so it is now time to realize you need to make decisions on your own. In an effort to try out your newfound independence, I have compiled a list, which I hope is helpful for you, as you take the next steps in your life post-divorce. Here are a few things that you need to do right away once the ink is dry and your ex is officially your ex. In no particular order, I recommend:

- <u>Get your money.</u> Make a list of all the payments that are due to you under your separation agreement or divorce decree and when these items should be delivered. If there are payments that are being made to you over time, such as deferred compensation payments that follow a vesting period, be sure to mark your calendar as to when those payments become due. Be sure to also keep track of all retirement accounts that need to be transferred as well.

- <u>One last divorce to-do list.</u> Compile a list of all the things you need to do on your end per the terms of the agreement. You may need to refinance the mortgage within thirty days of your agreement, or take his name off all the utility bills within a set amount of time. You also need to wipe his name from all your credit cards and transfer the bank accounts to your name or close the ones that have been tagged for closure.

- <u>Get a new will.</u> Odds are you have left everything and the kitchen sink to him if you were to get hit by a car tomorrow. Now, depending on the terms of your divorce and your current relationship with your ex, it is true that you may still want to leave him things in the event of your passing, or be required to leave certain funds. However, I doubt you want to leave him everything—so make changes to your estate-planning documents right away. Be sure to change your power of attorney too. If your divorce was acrimonious, I doubt you want him to be the one to decide if they pull the plug or not.

- <u>Change your user names and passwords.</u> Odds are he knows your password is your childhood pet's name, so be sure to change everything. You are wiping the slate clean and moving on—there is no need for him to be able to access any of your personal information anymore. He has lost that right and privilege.

- <u>Change your paperwork.</u> Assuming your agreement does not dictate otherwise, be sure to change your life insurance beneficiary, your retirement account beneficiaries, your bank and brokerage account beneficiaries (transfer upon death designations), and the like. If you have children, it is probably a wise idea that they benefit in the event you are not around. However, check with your attorney or financial adviser regarding setting up trusts for your kids if something were to happen to you and they are due funds. You do not want their father or some money-hungry new young wife to get their hands on cash that is rightfully the property of your children.

- <u>Switch your payment accounts.</u> Be sure you are clear about all the recurring bills you need to assume if your ex had been previously responsible. Determine if there were automatic payments that were being deducted from his bank account or charged to a credit card he has control over. In this event, you switch everything.

- <u>Create a new budget.</u> As stated, you are now in charge of your finances and you need to budget your money. So use the expense form your attorney gave you and fill it out again—this time figuring out what your expenses are going to be as you move forward. Do your best to maintain it and live within your means.

- <u>Find a financial planner.</u> Once you know how much money you are receiving, when you are being paid, and how much you are spending, you need to get a five-year, a ten-year, and a twenty-year financial plan in place. This type of plan is best devised with the help of a financial planner who can give you honest and level-headed advice. If you had a financial adviser you and your husband consulted previously, I will leave it up to you to determine if that person is still a viable option for you.

- <u>Get an accountant.</u> If you shared one with your ex prior to your divorce and are uncomfortable working with the same person now, you should definitely get a new one. An accountant is a powerful person to have in your arsenal of advisers—and their advice is valuable. Make sure this professional has all the information they need to help you.

- <u>Change your name.</u> If you have decided to change your name back to your maiden name, then you need to update your driver's license, Social Security card, and passport as well. Depending on your state, you usually have to start at the Social Security Administration with this name change, and then follow suit with other government agencies.

I encourage you to make sure you go through this list diligently and completely. Be sure to take this list and create a financial support team for yourself so you are primed and ready to focus on your life after divorce. However, if you have gotten through my list, then it is time to get on with your life!

DIVORCE PRESENTS

As a reward for completing your post-divorce to-do list and actually surviving your divorce—I recommend that you buy yourself a divorce present of some sort. Yes, it might seem like a splurge or a bit unnecessary as you adjust to a possible new financial situation, but seriously, you deserve it.

One of my favorite "divorce present" stories involves a woman—let's call her Kathy—who I represented when I first started practicing. Constantly mocked by her husband during their marriage for being flat-chested (he called her "Board" as a nickname—such an ass), it is easy to guess what she bought as soon as her big cash payment cleared. She is now the proud owner of D-cup bras! Still yet, I had another client who was the same height as her husband, and therefore, he was always upset whenever she would wear high heels. He was so insecure that he constantly insisted she wear flats. Post-divorce, her first stop after picking up her divorce judgment at my office was to Christian Louboutin, where she bought herself a fantastic pair of stilettos! (I often joke that my office is on Fifth Avenue simply because after people leave me, they can head straight uptown and go shopping—just call me the best divorce lawyer ever!)

Another great divorce success story involves a woman—let's call her Francine—whose husband was incredibly wealthy but also ridiculously cheap (which is probably how he became so wealthy). He was a businessman, and my client was a very talented homemaker—everything she touched was turned into a thing of beauty. Her home was exquisitely decorated and her holiday tables were breathtaking. She could throw a party like no one's business—but her husband would mock her, say her parties were silly, there were too many flowers in the house, and that she had no understanding of money. So one day while she and I were sitting in court for what felt like hours and hours, we discussed what she wanted to do after the divorce, and she told me how she loved to throw birthday parties. An idea bloomed and she started to consider throwing high-end tea parties for little girls on their birthdays. It was after the divorce and when she got her lump-sum payment that she started a business throwing these tea parties—and she became wildly successful. She ended up outearning her former husband! Talk about sweet revenge!

The moral of the story here is, whether it is new breasts, new shoes, or a new business, you need to do something for *you*. Plan a vacation (my office accepts credit card payments, so clients can earn airline miles and take a "divorcation" when it is all over), do a spa day, get a personal trainer, or do something you have dreamed about. I know the last umpteenth months have been about your kids, your ex, and your divorce—thus, "me" time is in order.

YOUR INNER MONOLOGUE

Once you have taken a bit of time and focused on your external desires or needs, it is then necessary to look inward and rediscover or reignite a positive inner monologue. Whether it is starting therapy (assuming you were not seeing someone during the whole divorce process) to figure out how to best deal with your new identity, trying a new hobby such as yoga, meditation, exercise, or even learning a new language, you need to do something that helps in the rebuilding process. There is going to be time to fill in the evenings and on the weekends—and therefore you need to find a way to take advantage of this new time opportunity and to keep your mind busy, engaged, and reinvigorated as you embark on the days ahead.

Now is your time to relaunch! Depending on your stage in life, you may not be experienced with the reality of the online-dating era. If this is the case, do not fear. While I advised you to stay off social media before, now is the time to take off those mittens and dust off the keyboard! I highly recommend beginning your new dating life by using many available online platforms. They are easy to use and can help you get back into the swing of dating. If you have been married for a long time and have not gone on a date in what feels like a zillion years, I encourage you to try to get excited about it. One of the great things about online-dating sites is that the odds of finding someone right away are slim (although it does happen!). Now, you may think, "Well, that sounds kind of depressing." Seriously though, it is not. Just like any skill, you need to relearn how to date, so you might as well practice on people who you do not have anything invested in. I would like you to hone your dating skills by experimenting on the masses who will be responding to your profile. Then, when you have your dating skills mastered, ask your best friend for setups, because there is a good chance this might end up being something real.

BEING SINGLE DOES NOT HAVE TO SUCK

While I know you may be insecure about dating again and think you cannot do it—I suggest you should try to look at things differently, if you can. When I was single, I loved dating. Many people cannot understand why I would say that, as it can be tedious, annoying, and exhausting. However, I looked at it differently. As you can imagine—since I chose the profession that I did—I admittedly find people intriguing. Therefore, I would date the starving artist who will never meet any of my friends and whose last name I would not even bother to remember. Why? Because I found speaking to him about the things I knew little about, or listening to how he experienced the world, was interesting. Do not look at every person you go out with as "the one" you are going to spend the rest of your life with. Give yourself some time to look around and meet different types of people. Allow yourself some time to learn about individuals who are outside your comfort zone. You may realize you do not find the artist interesting at all, or you may learn a thing or two that can broaden your perspective on life. Now, I will admit that the "dating strange people who only interest me for the night" game can get old eventually. And you may look for someone who is more of a keeper. But I do not recommend rushing into that.

When I dated (and even now when I go on networking "work dates"), I would often keep two stories in the back of my mind that I considered as my go-tos if a conversation started to get dull. The first story was usually a good work story that was a crowd-pleaser, and the other one was about an article I had recently read that would serve to stoke some conversation. Now, if it was a good date, I never had to utilize my back-up stories. If I ended up having to use backup story number two, we usually did not go out again. I am not recommending you script your dates, but I do advise you to have some per se "material" prepared if the restaurant's menu is more interesting than the conversation with your dinner companion.

Additionally, I would ask lots questions of my dates. Let's face it, everyone wants to talk about themselves. So on first dates, I would let them. First, I already know about me, so I felt no need to inform the other person on the subject—unless he asked. Second, it is so much easier when you do less of the talking, and your only requirement is to smile and nod and ask a few follow-up questions. Realize in this regard you do open yourself up to having to listen to boring stories and maybe a dumb joke or two, but at least you know after the first date whether you want to see that person again—hopefully, you were able to get a pretty accurate picture of who they are as a person. However, also remember to be an attentive listener, no matter how boring. Remember the kid in class who constantly raises her hand when the teacher is talking. That kid is not listening to the teacher, and only thinking about what she wants to say. People usually know if they are being heard. Unless he is so dry that you start creating the grocery shopping list in your head while he is talking about his cats and which flavored foods they prefer, try to pay attention. Moreover, this is a great test to see if the person realizes he is talking about himself the entire time—and if they are savvy enough to ask about you!

DINNER AND A MOVIE?

Gone are the days when you had to commit an entire evening to a date. We are busy people—unless it is warranted (or you really like the person), it is totally okay to be greedy and protective of your time if you are getting to know someone (or even multiple someones). Typically, I would start by meeting someone for a drink and then only graduate to dinner if there was chemistry and felt I could commit to a couple of hours with them. Which, by contrast, my friend would always want to go to dinner with dates because his theory was "I need to eat anyway, and if the date sucks at least I will have a good meal." Depending on your amount of free time, you can best decide how you want to structure first and second dates—just know there is not a rule to follow. If you have an hour for a drink, keep it to that hour. It is your time, and you are in charge of how you want to use it.

Assuming you have children already (or do not want children), then one of the nice things about dating after divorce is that you are no longer dating people who have to be "breeding material." You can date whomever you want! What I mean by that is, you have no pressure to find the father of your children anymore, so (depending on the age of your kids), this potential love interest can be someone you simply want to have fun with. Now, if you have younger kids who could be influenced by the people you date, then their suitability for your kids is a consideration. But if he has a big nose or bad teeth, you do not have to worry about the possibility of his DNA producing a child who you will need to get braces for or splurge on a nose job. It is time for you to enjoy romance with no strings attached. Now you can go back to being the fun and sexy woman you were before your energy and life were drained out of you from raising a handful of kids and living in a loveless, dysfunctional marriage. Because you are no longer a teenager, you will be wise about who you date, you will be safe, and you will clarify the rules before going into the game. But as long as you find someone who respects you and someone who will help you recover all the sensuality and femininity you might have lost along the way, by all means, date away!

There are studies that show once a person is freed from jail, said person will often commit another crime, just to go back. Despite how horrible a situation may be, there is comfort in what is familiar. Do not repeat the same mistakes you did before simply because they are comfortable. You are older and wiser than when you first married, so be aware of the warning signs related to getting into a relationship with someone who is like your ex. You need to be aware of patterns you want to avoid repeating, and work against the urge to return to what you know is not good for you just because you feel like it is what you know.

"MR. ONE NIGHT STAND, PLEASE MEET MY DAUGHTER, ALEXA." HOW TO INTRODUCE YOUR NEW GUY TO YOUR CHILDREN.

Let's say the dating thing worked out and you met someone great—and you are so excited and cannot wait for everyone to meet him because he is so great! While it is true a happy parent can make for happy children, it is necessary to be conscious about how a new partner can affect the dynamics with your kids. Deciding when and how to make an introduction between your significant other and your children must be done in a thoughtful manner where there is balance between all concerned parties—this includes you, your children, your new man, and yes, even your ex.

Timing is important

First, I would not recommend introducing your new love to your children until you are a thousand percent sure it is not going to cause a firestorm with your ex (if you can). An ideal situation is if your ex-husband has already entered into a relationship as well and has introduced your kids to his new girlfriend. In this regard, you have carte blanche to call the shots on how to handle the intro. If this is not the case, I encourage you to proceed with caution, but if there is never going to be a good time, then at least be sensitive about it.

Depending on your own situation, and if the split is amicable, there is a chance your divorce was calm and mutually accepted. If this is not the case, or if there were some acrimonious factors involved in your split, introducing the idea of a "new dad" to your kids could easily make your ex freak out. Realize that you can even significantly destroy a relatively cordial split by making your ex feel threatened by the fact there is some guy taking *his* place in *his* family. Now, considering your ex, it is true he might not want you anymore—but he does not want anyone else to have you either. And he especially does not like the idea of his children seeing some other man take care of you, walking the dog he trained, sitting in what used to be his space at the dinner table, or even (maybe if not today, then in the future) sleeping in the bed that he shared with you. Think how you would feel if your ex's new bombshell was in the position to take your daughter to the mall to go back-to-school shopping or pick your son up from baseball practice.

The point is: yes, think about your children—but also think about whether the timing is right with your ex.

See the situation through the eyes of others

No matter who was responsible for pulling the plug on your marriage, it is imperative that you take a step back and consider the situation through the perspective of your children's and your ex's eyes. Your kids are already dealing with the fact that Mom and Dad are not together anymore. How will they react when they see another man put his arm around you, hold your umbrella when it rains, open a car door, or even kiss you? I have mentioned that kids are very resilient. They have the ability to spring back from a variety of bad or challenging situations without suffering long-term damage. However, also know these little humans are very perceptive and sensitive—and remember they are also narcissistic.

Your kids have never seen you with anyone other than their father—and this could throw off their equilibrium. After all, if you have a new man in your life, does that mean you could possibly have new kids someday too? In the child's mind, you are their mom first, and that is the only identity that counts. Children can be just as possessive as your ex. Depending on the age of your child, their personality, and their relationship with their dad, they could experience some threatening feelings. They could challenge this new relationship, or look to undermine it. After all, how many times has the phrase "You are not my father!" been shouted on some TV drama featuring a blended family? Children often fantasize about their parents getting back together—and this new guy quashes that fantasy.

Also, remain aware that your child could experience feelings of abandonment, loss, or grief now that their dad is not around each day. Keep that in mind when you introduce a new love interest. You do not want your child to bond with this person, only to have him walk out on you a month later because he is not ready to commit or doesn't like the way you make your eggs in the morning. Ensure that the relationship is substantial before you spend your kids' time and emotions having them get to know and trust someone who might not be around a few months from now.

ACTIONABLE TIPS:
HOW TO MAKE THE INTRODUCTION

So now let us get to the part you have been waiting for. If you have established that, yes, it is time to make the introduction between your kids and your new boyfriend, here are some suggested how-to mechanics:

- If your child is in therapy, I would recommend speaking to your child's therapist about factors you should consider that pertain to your son's or daughter's individual needs. The therapist might have insight or best practices that could be applied to your child's personality, moods, challenges, or other issues surrounding your divorce.

- If your child is younger, have your new significant other be a "tag-along" person on a fun activity—like an amusement park or a trip to the zoo. Allow your child to feel like he had a really great day and hopefully, those fun feelings can start to be associated with your new friend.

- Involve your significant other in a nonintrusive way. He does not need to be the front-and-center attraction—rather, allow your child to interact with him in a way where trust and comfort can slowly be built.

- If your child is older, the "fun activity" might not work with them—and they could see through what you are trying to do (and probably call you out on it). Therefore, speak directly with them about your new relationship and let them dictate the terms of what would make them most comfortable when arranging this introduction.

You may be starting to recognize your new man could be a great addition or asset for your family, your child may not appreciate this just yet—it may take time and patience. Although you are understandably enthusiastic about your new partner, and all the possibilities this presents, your kid might be in a different place. Take conscious, levelheaded steps that support your parent-child relationship and help enable acceptance of your new partner. You might be ready to embrace the future, but know that your children could still be dealing with trying to achieve balance between their new reality and what your family looked like in the past. After you get them on board—then maybe you can accomplish the same thing with your ex.

A CHANCE TO ADVANCE IN YOUR CAREER

Being divorced and free is not all about dating and finding another man. I often encounter clients who fought tooth and nail to not give up their kids on the weeknights. When it did not work out in their favor, they have realized that instead, they might be able to take that time, stay late at work, and better their career. It is true it is very hard to balance parenthood and a career. That is why many people find when they do not have to be home to relieve the nanny by five o'clock or stay up all night making planet diorama school projects, they can focus more on work and move ahead in their careers. Your post-divorce life is offering you a chance to say yes to that project your boss has been dangling out there or go after the promotion you have been dreaming about. Seriously, the sky is the limit here—burn the midnight oil and realize your ex is not going to be at home nagging you or making you feel guilty about it.

THE GIFT OF FREE TIME—ENJOY IT

Divorce also opens up the opportunity to catch up with friends you have not seen—it can be a time to reconnect. This is also where social media can come in handy. The great thing about our digital world is that it is so easy to reach out to people from your past who you want to see but have never had the time. Take every other weekend when you are on your own to reconnect and broaden your friendship circles beyond your mommy friends, the DWC, and the other women in your circle of influence. There are great opportunities for growth now that you have been given some time to do so.

Also, use the time when your children are off with their father to try to get to the place where you can enjoy the quiet. It may be hard at first, but eventually you can get there. You can read the books you have been wanting to read, or do the art projects that seemed frivolous and silly when there was laundry to be done. Go see movies by yourself, or learn a new hobby.

Here is an opportunity to be free from having to answer to anyone but yourself (and maybe your kids). There is no guilt for spending a bunch of cash on a new bag because now you are in charge of your finances and only have to explain it to yourself. There will not be a critique or any complaints about eating crackers in bed as you are the one sleeping in the crumbs. Unless you personally enjoy it, you never have to suffer through football games on Sunday ever again. You are free to do what you want. So, live your life to its fullest! Buy yourself flowers. Sleep in incredibly late when your kids are at their father's. Have a one-night stand. Walk around naked when your kids are not there. Eat brownies directly from the pan as you watch reality TV. You are free to be who you are without judgment from a spouse and to do whatever you want. Learn to love yourself!

Of course, I am not trying to paint a picture that divorce is fun or that everyone should want to get divorced. But the message I am trying to get across is it is also not the worst thing that could have happened to you and could be a true blessing. There are silver linings. You may not know what they are as you sit here reading now, but one day I believe you will.

As crazy as it sounds, I love being a divorce attorney. People often ask me how I am able to do what I do for a living. They say, "Isn't it depressing, seeing marriages fall apart around you all the time?" The answer is no. I see divorce as the opportunity to transition out of the unhealthy relationship a person is in and position him/herself so he/she can enter a new healthy one. Personally, I feel honored I am in the position to help people get through one of the most difficult transitions they will ever face in their lives. On some level, and despite what I do for a living, I am still a true romantic and believe everyone can find their own happiness and their "someone." It is my hope that even after all you have been through with your divorce, you still believe that too.

ACKNOWLEDGMENTS

I would like to thank my editor Julia Cheiffetz for being a fantastic person and amazing publisher. I cannot express my gratitude to her for sharing my passion about getting a book out there that can really help people get through the difficult process of divorce. I also give much thanks to Julia's assistant editor, Nick Ciani, for answering my million-and-one questions, and the whole team at Atria Books, including Libby McGuire, Suzanne Donahue, Kristin Fassler, Joanna Pinsker, Shida Carr, and Isabel DaSilva. Thanks to my book agent, Kathy Schneider, for her support and enthusiasm and to David Gottlieb for introducing me to Kathy.

If not for my law partners Barry Berkman and Walter F. Bottger teaching me everything there was to know about matrimonial law and guiding me over the past twenty years, I never would have had the experience and knowledge to have written even one page of this book. To my law partner Evan Schein, who is always so supportive—thank you for thinking big with me.

Thanks to everyone at Berkman Bottger Newman & Schein for making me want to go to work (almost) every day.

To all my family and friends, I am lucky to have you in my life.

To Matthew, Rachael, Jake, and Elena Lipson, who had to listen to me go on and on about this book over our many family vacations and be understanding when I had to take out my laptop to work while at your BBQs.

Lots of love and appreciation must go to my husband, Jarrod Newman. Being married to a divorce attorney definitely has its risks, but you took the chance anyway. Thanks for taking the gamble, killing bugs, being up for anything, always being proud of me and, of course, your love and support (but mostly the bug killing).

To my daughters, Samantha and Alexandra Newman, I love you both so much and cherish being your Mom. You can accomplish anything you put your minds to (except beating me at gin rummy). Remember the sky is not the limit if you reach for the stars.

And finally, I want to thank my parents, Beverly and Leonard Lipson, for . . . basically everything. But especially my Mom—who was my original editor and has always been my biggest cheerleader. Your unconditional love has given me power.

NOTES

INTRODUCTION

1 Rebecca Lake, "How Long Do Average U.S. Marriages Last?" *The Balance*, June 25, 2019, https://www.thebalance.com/how-long-do-average-u-s-marriages-last -4590261.

SECRET #1: DIVORCE, LIKE MARRIAGE, IS A NEW WORLD WITH NEW RULES

1 Claire Cain Miller and Quoctrung Bui, "Equality in Marriages Grows, and So Does Class Divide." *New York Times*, February 27, 2016, https://www.nytimes.com/2016 /02/23/upshot/rise-in-marriages-of-equals-and-in-division-by-class.html.

2 "Labor Force Statistics from the Current Population Survey: Wives who earn more than their husbands, 1987–2011," United States Department of Labor, Bureau of Labor Statistics, November 20, 2012, http://web.archive.org/web /20140207135501/https://www.bls.gov/cps/wives_earn_more.htm.

3 Mona Chalabi, "How Many Women Earn More Than Their Husbands?" FiveThirtyEight, February 5, 2015, https://fivethirtyeight.com/features/how -many-women-earn-more-than-their-husbands/.

4 https://www.urbandictionary.com/define.php?term=sahd.

5 Marianne Bertrand, Emir Kamenica, and Jessica Pan, "Gender Identity and Relative Income within Households," *Quarterly Journal of Economics* 130, no. 2 (2015): 571–614. doi:10.1093/qje/qjv001.

6 Chalabi, "How Many Women Earn More Than Their Husbands?"

7 Ibid.

8 Marta Murray-Close and Misty L. Heggeness, *Manning Up and Womaning*

245

Down: How Husbands and Wives Report Their Earnings When She Earns More, United States Census Bureau, Social, Economic, and Housing Statistics Division, SESHD Working Paper # 2018-20, June 6, 2018. https://www.census.gov/content /dam/Census/library/working-papers/2018/demo/SEHSD-WP2018-20.pdf.

9   Ibid.

10 Jillian Berman, "When Wives Earn More than Their Husbands, They Both Do Something Pretty Terrible," *MarketWatch*, July 26, 2018, https://www.market watch.com/story/when-wives-earn-more-than-their-husbands-they-both-lie -2018-07-18.

11 Mona Chalabi, "What Happens When Wives Earn More Than Husbands," interview by Rachel Martin, *Weekend Edition Sunday*, NPR, February 8, 2015, https:// www.npr.org/2015/02/08/384695833/what-happens-when-wives-earn-more -than-husbands.

12 Jacklynn N. Price v. Harold Price, 69 N.Y.2d 511 (1986).

13 Gretchen Livingston, "The Changing Profile of Unmarried Parents," Pew Research Center, Social & Demographic Trends, April 25, 2018, https://www.pew socialtrends.org/2018/04/25/the-changing-profile-of-unmarried-parents/.

14 "How Much Custody Time Does Dad Get in Your State?" Custody X Change, June 5, 2018, https://www.custodyxchange.com/maps/dads-custody-time-2018.php.

15 Center for Applied Research in the Apostolate. "Divorce (Still) Less Likely Among Catholics." *Nineteen Sixty-Four*, September 26, 2013. http://nineteen sixty-four.blogspot.com/2013/09/divorce-still-less-likely-among.html.

16 *Catechism of the Catholic Church—IntraText*, accessed August 6, 2019. http:// www.vatican.va/archive/ENG0015/_P87.HTM.

SECRET #3: YOU NEED TO PUT ON YOUR OWN
OXYGEN MASK FIRST—SELF-CARE IS KEY

1   Reese Witherspoon, "Reese Witherspoon: The actress on heartbreak, hard work, and her latest movie," *ELLE*, March 4, 2009, https://www.elle.com/culture/celeb rities/a9039/reese-witherspoon-307443/.

SECRET #4: YOU ARE NOT
DIVORCING THE SAME PERSON YOU MARRIED

1   Tracy Smith, "What Is the Grey Rock Method," eCounseling, April 26, 2009, https://www.google.com/amp/s/www.e-counseling.com/mental-health/what-is -the-grey-rock-method/amp/.

SECRET #5: YOU DO NOT NEED TO SEE
THE INSIDE OF A COURTROOM TO GET DIVORCED

1   Law, Weinberger Divorce & Family. "Divorce Secrets of the Rich & Famous." *Weinberger Divorce & Family Law Group*. Weinberger Divorce & Family Law

https://www.weinbergerlawgroup.com/wp-content/uploads/2017/04/wlg
-logo@2x.png, July 14, 2017. Weinberger Divorce & Family Law Group, "Divorce
Secrets of the Rich & Famous," December 15, 2013, https://www.weinbergerlaw
group.com/blog/newjersey-divorce-mediation/divorce-secrets-of-the-rich-fa
mous/.

2 Jeff Landers, "Divorcing Women: Is It Best to Litigate or Settle?" *Forbes*, May 22,
2014, https://www.forbes.com/sites/jefflanders/2014/05/22/divorcing-women
-is-it-best-to-litigate-or-settle/amp/.

SECRET #7: NEITHER OF YOU
ARE AS WEALTHY AS YOU THOUGHT

1 John L. Smith, "Casino Mogul Steve Wynn Won't Let His Ex-Wife Control Her
$1 Billion in Stock," *Daily Beast*, May 31, 2016, updated April 13, 2017, https://
www.thedailybeast.com/casino-mogul-steve-wynn-wont-let-his-ex-wife-con
trol-her-dollar1-billion-in-stock.

2 Ken Lee, "Mel Gibson's Divorce Could Be Most Expensive in Hollywood History," *People*, April 14, 2009, https://people.com/celebrity/mel-gibsons-divorce
-could-be-most-expensive-in-hollywood-history/.

3 Meredith Blake and Meg James, "Rupert Murdoch, Wendi Murdoch Announce
Divorce Settlement," *Los Angeles Times*, November 20, 2013, https://www.latimes
.com/entertainment/envelope/cotown/la-et-ct-rupert-murdoch-wendi-deng
-murdoch-divorce-settlement-20131120-story.html.

SECRET #8: YOUR SUPPORT AWARDS
MAY NOT ACTUALLY SUPPORT YOU

1 "Facts Over Time—Women in the Labor Force," U.S. Department of Labor,
Women's Bureau, accessed August 6, 2019, https://www.dol.gov/wb/stats/NEW
STATS/facts/women_lf.htm#CivilianLFSex.

2 "Economic News Release: Table A-1. Employment Status of the Civilian Population by Sex and Age," United States Department of Labor, Bureau of Labor Statistics," August 2, 2019, https://www.bls.gov/news.release/empsit.t01.htm.

3 "TED: The Economics Daily. Educational Attainment of Women in the Labor
Force, 1970–2010," United States Department of Labor, Bureau of Labor
Statistics, December 29, 2011, https://www.bls.gov/opub/ted/2011/ted_20111
229.htm.

4 Mark DeWolf, "12 Stats About Working Women," U.S. Department of Labor
Blog, March 1, 2017, https://blog.dol.gov/2017/03/01/12-stats-about-working
-women.

5 "Labor Force Statistics from the Current Population: Employed Persons by De-
tailed Occupation, Sex, Race, and Hispanic or Latino Ethnicity," United States
Department of Labor, Bureau of Labor Statistics, January 18, 2019, https://www
.bls.gov/cps/cpsaat11.htm.

6 Geoff Williams, "More Men Get Alimony from Their Ex-Wives," Reuters, December 24, 2013, https://www.reuters.com/article/us-divorce-alimony-men /more-men-get-alimony-from-their-ex-wives-idUSBRE9BN0AW20131224.

7 "Big Increase of Women Paying Alimony and Child Support," American Academy of Matrimonial Lawyers, May 14, 2018, http://web.archive.org/web /20190517031321/http://aaml.org/about-the-academy/press/press-releases/big -increase-women-paying-alimony-and-child-support.

SECRET #9: FIFTY-FIFTY
CUSTODY IS BECOMING THE NORM

1 Susanna N. Visser, Melissa L. Danielson, Rebecca H. Bitsko, Joseph R. Holbrook, Michael D. Kogan, Reem M. Ghandour, Ruth Perou, and Stephen J. Blumberg, "Trends in the Parent-Report of Health Care Provider-Diagnosed and Medicated Attention-Deficit/Hyperactivity Disorder: United States, 2003–2011," *Journal of the American Academy of Child & Adolescent Psychiatry* 53, no. 1 (2014): 34–46. doi:10.1016/j.jaac.2013.09.001.

2 Ibid.

SECRET #10: YOUR CHILDREN MAY
BE BETTER OFF AFTER YOUR DIVORCE

1 Kimberly Howard and Richard V. Reeves. "The Marriage Effect: Money or Parenting?" *Brookings*, September 4, 2014, https://www.brookings.edu/research /the-marriage-effect-money-or-parenting/.

2 Ibid.

3 Stephanie Chen, "Children of Divorce Vow to Break Cycle, Create Enduring Marriages," CNN, September 22, 2010, http://web.archive.org/web/20170910032314 /https://www.cnn.com/2010/LIVING/09/22/divorced.parents.children.mar riage/.

SECRET #11: YOU MAY BE IN AN
ABUSIVE MARRIAGE AND NOT EVEN KNOW IT

1 Michele C. Black, Kathleen C. Basile, Matthew J. Breiding, Sharon G. Smith, Mikel L. Walters, Melissa T. Merrick, Jieru Chen, and Mark R. Stevens, *The National Intimate Partner and Sexual Violence Survey: 2010 Summary Report*. Atlanta, GA: National Center for Injury Prevention and Control, Centers for Disease Control and Prevention, November 2011, https://www.cdc.gov/violence prevention/pdf/nisvs_report2010-a.pdf.

2 Jennifer L. Truman and Rachel E. Morgan, *Nonfatal Domestic Violence, 2003– 2012*, Office of Justice Programs, U.S. Department of Justice, April 2014, https:// www.bjs.gov/content/pub/pdf/ndv0312.pdf.

3 Jacquelyn C. Campbell, Daniel Webster, Jane Koziol-McLain, Carolyn Block,

Doris Campbell, Mary Ann Curry, Faye Gary, et al., "Risk Factors for Femicide in Abusive Relationships: Results From a Multisite Case Control Study," *American Journal of Public Health* 93, no. 7 (2003): 1089–97. doi:10.2105/ajph.93.7.1089.

4 Truman and Morgan. *Nonfatal Domestic Violence.*

5 Sherry Hamby, David Finkelhor, Heather A. Turner, and Richard Ormrod, *Children's Exposure to Intimate Partner Violence and Other Family Violence.* Office of Juvenile Justice and Deliquency Prevention, Office of Justice Programs, U.S. Department of Justice, October 2011, https://www.ncjrs.gov/pdffiles1/ojjdp /232272.pdf.

6 L. Vargas, J. Cataldo, and S. Dickson, "Domestic Violence and Children," in *VISTAS: Compelling Perspectives on Counseling*, eds. G. R. Walz, K. Yep (Alexandria, VA: American Counseling Association, 2005), 67–69.

7 "The Facts on Children and Domestic Violence," Futures Without Violence, August 2008, https://www.futureswithoutviolence.org/userfiles/file/Children_and _Families/Children.pdf.

8 Emily DeSanctis, "What Emotional Abuse Really Means," One Love, https:// www.joinonelove.org/learn/emotional-abuse-really-means/.

9 Adam M. Tomison and Joe Tucci, "Emotional Abuse: The Hidden Form of Maltreatment," Australian Institute of Family Studies, September 1997, https://aifs .gov.au/cfca/publications/emotional-abuse-hidden-form-maltreatment#def.

10 James Garbarino, Edna Guttmann, and Janis Wilson Seeley. *The Psychologically Battered Child: Strategies for Identification, Assessment and Intervention* (San Francisco: Jossey-Bass, 1986).

11 Black et al., *National Intimate Partner and Sexual Violence Survey.*

12 Kelly J. Kelleher, William Gardner, Jeff Coben, Rick Barth, Jeff Edleson, Andrea Hazen, *Co-occurring Intimate Partner Violence and Child Maltreatment: Local Policies/Practices and Relationships to Child Placement, Family Services and Residence*, National Institute of Justice, Grant Number 2002-WG-BX0014, March 2006, https://www.ncjrs.gov/pdffiles1/nij/grants/213503.pdf.